At once pragmatic and idealistic, Jaspers gives America's swollen and overburdened universities a constructive, cogent answer to the current debate between those who favor increasing specialization and those who champion general education.

About the author:

Professor Karl Jaspers is equally outstanding as an authority on philosophy, psychiatry, and literature. He is known throughout the academic world as an exponent of Existentialism, and as one of the greatest figures in German university life, who refused to support Hitler and continued to stand by his refusal inside Germany throughout the Nazi reign. After the defeat of Hitler, Jaspers was one who forced German academicians to face the inescapable responsibility for their own share of guilt in bowing to Hitler. At present he is Professor of Philosophy at the University of Basel, Switzerland.

His numerous writings include *Tragedy Is Not Enough,* published by the Beacon Press as an earlier volume in this *Seeds-of-Thought* series.

THE IDEA OF THE UNIVERSITY

SEEDS-OF-THOUGHT SERIES

edited by Karl W. Deutsch

Relativity—A Richer Truth, by Philipp Frank, with a foreword by Albert Einstein

The Idea of the University, by Karl Jaspers

Tragedy Is Not Enough, by Karl Jaspers

German History: Some New German Views, edited by Hans Kohn

Freedom Is the Right to Choose, by Archibald MacLeish

The State Versus Socrates, edited with an introduction by John D. Montgomery

The Driving Power of Western Civilization, by Eugen Rosenstock-Huessy

also edited by Karl W. Deutsch (with H. T. Moore)

The Human Prospect, by Lewis Mumford

THE IDEA
OF THE UNIVERSITY

By Karl Jaspers

Edited by Karl W. Deutsch

Preface by Robert Ulich

Translated by H. A. T. Reiche
and H. F. Vanderschmidt

Beacon Press   Beacon Hill   Boston

This book was previously published in German under the title,
Die Idee der Universität.

To

KARL HEINRICH BAUER

Professor of Surgery

President of Heidelberg University

and in charge of its reconstruction

In Friendship and Gratitude

Biographical Note

Karl Jaspers was born in Oldenburg, Germany in 1883. Equally outstanding as an authority on philosophy, psychiatry, and literature, he is perhaps best known as an exponent of Existentialism. One of the greatest figures in German university life, he taught philosophy at the University of Heidelberg from 1921 until his suspension by the Nazis in 1937. He refused to support Hitler and continued to stand by his refusal within Germany throughout the Nazi regime. Spared from scheduled deportation by the entry of the U. S. Army, he was reinstated in 1945 as University President and elected Honorary Senator of the University in 1946. Since 1948 he has been Professor of Philosophy at the University of Basel, Switzerland.

Among his other works are: *Psychologie der Weltanschauungen* (1919); *Die geistige Situation der Zeit* (1931) (translated as *Man in the Modern Age*); *Existenzphilosophie* (1938); *Die Schuldfrage: ein Beitrag zur deutschen Frage* (1946) (translated as *The Question of German Guilt*); and *Der Philosophische Glaube* (1948) (translated as *The Perennial Scope of Philosophy*).

A major work, *Von der Wahrheit* (1947) still awaits translation. A section of this work has been translated as *Tragedy Is Not Enough*.

Contents

Editor's Note: Jaspers' Challenge to the Universities   ix

Preface by Robert Ulich: On Jaspers' Philosophy of Existence and Education   xv

INTRODUCTION   1

PART I: *The Intellectual Life*   5

CHAPTER 1: *The Nature of Science and Scholarship*   7

Basic Characteristics of Science and Scholarship, 7—The Narrower and the Wider Concept of Science, 8—The Limits of Science, 13—Science as Utilitarian *versus* Science as an End in Itself, 14—The Basic Assumptions of Science, 17—Science Needs Direction, 20—Science as the Presupposition of Truthfulness, 23—Science and Philosophy, 25

CHAPTER 2: *Spirit, Human Existence, Reason*   28

CHAPTER 3: *Culture*   30

PART II: *The Objectives of the University*   37

CHAPTER 4: *Research, Education and Instruction*   39

Research, 41—Education as Formation of the Mind, 48—Instruction, 56

CHAPTER 5: *Communication*   62

Debate and Discussion, 64—The Formation of "Schools of Thought" as an Instance of Intellectual Cooperation, 65—The University as the Meeting Place of Different Disciplines and World Outlooks, 67

CHAPTER 6: *The University as an Institution*   70

The Failure of the Institution to Live Up to the Idea of the University, 70—The Necessity for Institutions, 74—The Role of Personality within the Formal Structure of the University, 77

CHAPTER 7: *The Cosmos of Knowledge*   80

The Classification of Knowledge, 81—Academic Departments, 84—The Expansion of the University, 88

PART III: *The Requisites for the Existence of the University*   99

CHAPTER 8: *The Human Factor*   101

Types of Aptitude, 102—The Distribution of Aptitudes and the Characteristics of the Masses, 107—The Process of Selection, 111

CHAPTER 9: *State and Society*   121

The University as a State within the State, 121—Changes in the University in a Changing World, 122—The Meaning of Government Supervision, 123—The Principle of an Intellectual Aristocracy, 128—The Search for Truth and Its Relation to Politics, 130—The University and the Nation, 134

Editor's Note

Karl Jaspers' *The Idea of the University* was written at the end of Hitler's dictatorship and the defeat of Germany in World War II, after the worst outward and inner catastrophies had befallen the German universities. The outward destruction was evident in the rubble of the German cities. The inner devastation was less manifest but worse. It was the memory of the thousands of students who had forsaken the books of Kant for the loudspeakers of Goebbels and the jackboots of the elite guards; the professors who had eagerly believed the nationalistic and racial propaganda, forsaking their standards of critical thinking; and those other professors who, while not believing the doctrines of the Third Reich, yet found it prudent to pretend belief, and not deceived, yet aided the deceivers.

Amidst this moral ruin, a minority of German students and teachers held firm to their commitments to honesty and independent thought. Many of them paid for this commitment with their lives, or with years in concentration camps or exile. Still others, like Karl Jaspers, lived in Germany, nominally free but barred from teaching, and in constant danger. These students and professors preserved and redeemed the honor of the German universities in one of the most terrible periods of testing that any community of students and scholars ever had to meet.

Karl Jaspers, we know, was one of these people. But he did more. He was one of the first after the collapse of the nightmare empire of the Nazis to call to reconstruction—to the rebuilding of the German universities from their foundations. He offered a philosopher's search for the deepest roots and the innermost core of those strange human enterprises that we call universities in the tradition of the Western World. In so doing, he showed in a brief sample the continuing vitality and greatness of the German philosophic tradition: he wrote a pamphlet for his time and place, the shattered Germany of 1946, and at the same time a deep-probing statement for many times and many places.

His views have a contribution to offer to our own unending American debate about the nature and function of higher education in this country. We are committed in this country to make higher education available ultimately to all of our people capable to benefit from it. But in moving toward this goal we must be concerned that this higher education should not become diluted or debased in the process. More than ever, we must try to preserve and strengthen its essentials; and we have reason to attend to a philosopher's advice as to what these essentials are.

If we thus listen to Jaspers, we may sometimes find ourselves surprised. Some of his ideas may shock us, or strike us as impractical or worse. Yet even those most at variance with the practices at many of our own universities may deserve a thoughtful hearing.

Jaspers believes that in any true university three things—academic teaching, scientific and scholarly research, and creative cultural life—are indissolubly linked to each other; and that each of these activities will wither and decline in the long run if separated from the others. Thus to Jaspers, an increase in the numbers of full-time research men and full-time teachers at a university would bring forebodings of intellectual decline; and he insists that no man who is not himself carrying on research can truly teach and educate students at a university.

In his philosophy, Jaspers has been an uncompromising enemy of fascism and communism. While refusing any intellectual concessions to the adversaries of freedom, he insists on continuing communication at the level of the university without any political or ideological curtains. Not out of any naïve ignorance of political reality, but due to firsthand ex-

perience of twelve years under a totalitarian tyranny, Jaspers
believes that a university must remain committed to such free
intellectual communication, and hence that into its community
it should

> even admit people who have made what is called the *sacrificio
> del intelletto* (the sacrifice of the intellect): even those who
> would be intolerant if they could. The university feels con-
> fident that it can afford to do so. It wants to live dynamically,
> not statically. In its will to communicate it seeks to associate
> even with those who resist communication. It would be con-
> trary to the idea of the university to deny admission to a man
> of intellectual rank who shows proof of intellectual achievement
> and works in a scholarly way—even if his scholarship ultimately
> serves an alien interest.

He carefully qualifies his point:

> The demand that every world outlook be represented at the
> university, for example in philosophy, history, sociology and
> political science, is just as unsuited to the idea of the university.
> If a given world outlook fails to produce scholars of the first
> rank, then this outlook has no claim to scientific status. The
> individual certainly prefers living together with those who
> share his ideas. As long as he acknowledges the idea of the
> university and has a voice in the selection of candidates for
> admission, however, he will be inclined to draw the most
> diverse viewpoints into the university. He does this in order
> to create opportunities for fruitful conflict to broaden the intel-
> lectual range at whatever risk—above all, to allow scholarly
> achievement and intellectual quality alone to be the decisive
> factors. The university not only tolerates but demands that
> persons who oppose its aims be admitted to it. So long as these
> people are content to state and discuss their particular beliefs
> and authorities within the university, so long as they allow their
> beliefs to be an impulse for their research, they are useful to
> the university. But if they seek to dominate the university with
> these beliefs, if in the selection of candidates for the university
> they are partial to fellow-believers, if they replace intellectual

freedom by prophetic propaganda, then they come into the
sharpest of conflict with the rest of the university which aims
to uphold the ideal of the university.

It is easy to think of arguments against these views. Such
counter-arguments will seem strongest against the background
of some current emergency or crisis, some war or near-war
situation, where all long-range principles seem overshadowed
by the need for expediency in meeting the danger of the moment. Yet, as crisis follows upon crisis, our minds and institutions will require longer views and deeper thoughts.

In a world of many and long-lasting emergencies we still
must think about our higher education not only in terms of
the need of the present and the short-run future, but also in
terms of the long-run future as it seems illuminated by the
experiences of the long-run past. No totalitarian dictatorship
has lasted for three generations, but the institution of the relatively free universities of the Western World has endured by
now for almost nine hundred years, with a record of almost
unparalleled vitality and growth. If we wish this growth to
continue, we may well ask what has been its secret; and Karl
Jaspers' attempt at a philosophic answer may well be relevant
to some of the decisions that face all of us, citizens, students,
and teachers, here and now.

The present translation includes all of the German book,
except for the last part of the ninth chapter and the whole of
the tenth. The omitted passages, corresponding to pages 124-
132 of the original, refer to conditions specific to Germany or
to the immediate post-war situation of 1946, and are not
directly relevant to American conditions.

A brief discussion of Jaspers' approach, by a philosopher
of education thoroughly familiar with conditions in the United
States, will be found immediately following in the "Preface"
by Professor Robert Ulich.

Further notes on Jaspers, a bibliography of his writings
to 1952, and a discussion by Professor Harald A. T. Reiche, of

Jaspers' style and the problems of its translation into English, are contained in another small volume of Jaspers' writings, *Tragedy Is Not Enough,* in this same "Seeds-of-Thought" series and published by the Beacon Press.

Yale University   KARL W. DEUTSCH

Preface

Karl Jaspers, together with Martin Heidegger, is Germany's leading representative of "existentialism." Certainly, a man of his ceaselessly inquiring mind is indifferent to finding his ideas and reputation affixed with a fashionable label, particularly if that label is used to denote so many varieties of philosophical thought that it is often more confusing than clarifying. Still, he himself chose the title *Existenzphilosophie: Three Lectures* (Walter de Gruyter, 1938) for one of his best-known publications.

At a time when German academic philosophy was primarily interested in the highly technical subtleties of "Neo-Kantianism," Jaspers became profoundly concerned with an issue far more comprehensive than mere theory of knowledge (though by no means unrelated to it), namely that of the human being and his ultimate relation to himself and the universe. "What is called Philosophy of Existence"—he says in his above-mentioned lectures—"is but a new form of the one and perennial philosophy.

"The fact that 'existence' has now become a word of central significance is not merely accidental. For it emphasizes the almost forgotten purpose of philosophy, namely, *to intuit and comprehend the origin and essence of reality by the mode in which, as a thinking person, and in a kind of inward-directed action, I am concerned with understanding my own individual existence.* This form of philosophizing intends to find a way back to that which really is, away from the mere knowing *about* the world, away from the customary fashions of speaking, from conventions and the playing of parts—away from all that is mere foreground and surface. *Existence* is one of the concepts which points toward reality, with the accent given it by Kierkegaard; only by virtue of being fully myself can I grasp the truth of reality."

Several influences led Jaspers to this depth of philosophical concern. In consequence of our modern tendency to enclose the work of scholars into departmental boxes, an impressive and important fact in Jaspers' career has remained rather unknown, namely that—after studying jurisprudence and medicine—he began his professional career as a psychiatrist.* He is the author of one of the best-known German textbooks in this field (*Allgemeine Psychopathologie*) which after 1913 went quickly through several editions and was also translated into French. This training not only enabled him in his treatise on *The Idea of the University* to write competently about the scientific responsibilities of higher education, but also—and perhaps more important, it sharpened his insight into the transphysical layers of human existence; hence his frequent emphasis on the greatness, yet also the limitations of empirical science. Another source of influence came from his encounter with the two thinkers who, probably more than any others, during the nineteenth century, had asked the most radical questions (though from the opposite point of view) about man's relationship to himself, his civilization, his society, and the Ultimate: the Danish theologian, Soeren Kierkegaard, and the German philosopher, Friedrich Nietzsche.

But to characterize Jaspers, or any other original thinker, with reference solely to influences he underwent during the formative phase of his philosophy would be partial and one-sided. For every creative mind not only transforms suggestions and inspirations from outside during the process of absorption, however gratefully he may acknowledge them, but he also expands his search toward directions inherent in his own

* Jaspers himself has written an intellectual autobiography the English translation of which, with the title On My Philosophy, is contained in *Existentialism from Dostoevsky to Sartre*, selected and introduced by Walter Kaufmann (New York: Meridian Books, 1956) and, even more recently, the lengthy Autobiography especially written for the volume, *The Philosophy of Karl Jaspers*, the Library of Living Philosophers, ed. P. Schilpp (New York: Tudor, 1957).

work and personality. The sheer volume of writings which Jaspers, now aged seventy-four, can look back upon is enormous, ranging (to mention only his philosophical investigations) all the way from studies of the psychological bases of the great systems of thought to modern epistemological problems, and from analyses of individual personalities, e.g. Nietzsche, to comprehensive syntheses dealing with the meaning of civilizations and of human history as a whole.

Who is better qualified to write on the idea and the ideals of higher education than a man of such intellectual breadth?

It would be preposterous to use this introduction to summarize for the reader what he will be reading for himself. Only two remarks may be appropriate here.

First, though in *The Idea of the University* Jaspers does not speak expressly of existential philosophy, the informed reader senses the existentialist quest. On the first page the leitmotif of the whole book is stated: the university is the place where man has the freedom to search for truth and to teach truth in defiance of anyone who wishes to curtail this freedom. To paraphrase Jaspers' definition of existential philosophy (given above), the university is a place where man must be allowed to find himself through authentic thinking and living, "away from the customary modes of speaking, from conventions and the playing of parts—away from all that is mere foreground and surface."

Second, in emphasizing the role of the university as the community of the guardians of truth, Jaspers aligns himself with that tradition which had accounted for the greatness of the German university ever since Kant wrote his treatise on *The Strife of Faculties* (*Der Streit der Fakultäten,* 1798), and the theologian Schleiermacher, who so deeply influenced liberal religion in Europe and the United States, wrote his essay on the spirit of the university (*Gelegentliche Gedanken über Universitäten,* 1808).

Though Germany may claim that, at the turn of the eighteenth century, it was the first of the European countries to take seriously the demand for the freedom of thought which Spinoza had raised in his *Tractatus Theologico-Politicus* of 1670, it is by no means Germany alone from which great documents on the ideal function of the university have issued. After the long suppression of academic liberty in France under the ancient regime, the revolution and Napoleon, two French authors, Victor Cousin and Ernest Renan, both influenced by German thought, restored the dignity of French higher education about and after the middle of the nineteenth century. In England, about the same time Oxford and Cambridge were awakening from a long and comfortable slumber, Cardinal Newman wrote his famous treatise on *The Idea of a University Defined and Illustrated* (1859). And two years before Karl Jaspers published the second edition of the essay here translated, there appeared *The Mission of the University* by Ortega y Gasset (1944), a Spaniard who could no longer be at home in his own fatherland but had to choose the whole world for his domain of living and intellectual exchange.

But here one cannot suppress a sad reflection. With all these high ideals in their tradition, how could it happen that, despite the courageous resistance of some professors the universities of so many European countries collapsed shamefully under the attacks of dictators?

One reason, of course, is the cruelty and thoroughness of strategy by which totalitarian governments pursue their destructive aims against human freedom. Universities have no guns and armies, and whether lawfully or not, they can be closed and silenced.

Another reason, however, is that, with few exceptions, the European university professor cared too little about the interaction between academic life and its social and political environment. And this, it seems to me, applied especially to the German scholar, however great his merits in other respects.

He could indeed feel himself protected by a long and sacred tradition and forever shielded by a benevolent and respectful government. In addition, he enjoyed high social prestige and, when he "arrived"—which, of course, was not easy—even a high income. Thus he did not understand that the price of freedom is vigilance and readiness for sacrifice; he took his exalted position for granted and did not see, or did not want to see, the clouds growing darker and darker above the academic world.

Still, provided an ideal corresponds to the true aims of man, it is not any less true because it has sometimes been deserted by weak human beings. If goals never fully attainable did not exist as a challenge and spur to man's conscience, the frontiers of civilization would never have been pushed forward. And while, to the dismay of intellectual Germany, some of Karl Jaspers' famous philosophical colleagues betrayed their own professed ideals under the impact of National Socialism, he himself stood upright. Even when his life was in danger, he represented the kind of person upon whom the Romans would have bestowed the title *vir fortis et constans*, "brave and steadfast man." He not only talked about truth: he lived in truth, as he had always demanded it from everyone who wished to be counted a man with a sense for true and authentic living.

It is not easy to translate any of Jaspers' works. Needless to say, *The Idea of the University* has been rendered into English not merely to add one more book to the ever-swelling number of treatises on higher education. We should listen to it as the voice of a man who, after years of suppression and suffering, could again express his belief in the lasting, and ultimately irrepressible, value of truth, and we should use it as a spur to look critically upon our own situation.

We may see a certain safeguard against governmental tyranny in the decentralization of the American school system and the independence of so many of our leading academic

institutions from state departments and political parties. On
the other hand, we are not always happy about the dependence of our colleges and universities on private donors, which
forces our presidents to knock at the doors of rich men not
genuinely interested in academic freedom, sometimes perhaps
even suspicious of it. We still remember the hearings presided
over by Senator McCarthy in the early 1950's. Our administrative staffs grow from year to year to take care of public relations and the avalanche of petty responsibilities. We sometimes despair of our capacity to instill in the ever-growing
masses of students, perhaps even in our own colleagues, a sense
for those values of higher education that are more than merely
utilitarian. We wonder how much room may still be left for
the virtues of contemplation which are the prerequisites of
creative scholarship. We may also ask ourselves the painful
question—how our colleges and universities would stand the
test of battle against dictatorships. Some, we know, have failed
even before minor powers.

Nor is it enough to say that many of their apparent disad-
vantages which keep our places of learning in contact with the
vicissitudes and sharp edges of the practical world—and these
are not always pleasant experiences—may be, at least in part,
our empirical way of learning about, and living within, "the
origin and essence of reality."

But perhaps it is not our intrinsic merit, but our more
fortunate historical and political situation that has permitted
us to survive. To be sure, during the past thirty years a whole
flood of literature has arisen about the value of the liberal arts
and the relationship between the sciences and the humanities,
and we may rightly interpret this as a sign of our own urge
for self-examination. Thank heaven, we have even the courage
to laugh heartily at our weaknesses.

Yet we have little that, with good conscience, we could
set at the side of the works of Schleiermacher, Newman,
Ortega y Gasset or Jaspers. Of our more than fifteen hundred

colleges, many cannot claim to have made any contribution to creative scholarship. There are reasons: it has been not much more than two generations since the American institutions of higher learning have risen above the older type of college, which was a sort of middle ground between secondary and truly academic learning. We still show the traces of the older conditions in our desire to guide the student through every step of his career, to prescribe his reading, and to control his progress through a pedantic process of examinations. All this is far from the idea of higher learning as expressed by the men just mentioned.

In addition, though we have individual manifestoes of power and significance by some of our great university presidents, they were more concerned with educational policy than with philosophical problems. Moreover, we like to work in committees. Though such labor may be effective from a practical point of view, it ends by necessity in compromising ultimate issues and deeper convictions, if not in avoiding them totally. "Existentialist" questions are rarely asked in "Reports."

It matters little what term we may choose to denote reality. Indeed, existentialism has no monopoly in this respect. But only if this struggle will be valiantly fought and expressed can higher education and the democratic society find the sources of continual inner re-creation and heightened productivity.

Harvard University   ROBERT ULICH

THE IDEA OF THE UNIVERSITY

INTRODUCTION

The university is a community of scholars and students engaged in the task of seeking truth. It is a body which administers its own affairs regardless of whether it derives its means from endowments, ancient property rights or the state; or whether its original public sanction comes from papal bulls, imperial charters or the acts of provinces or states. In every case its independent existence reflects the express wish or continuing toleration on the part of the founder. Like the church it derives its autonomy—respected even by the state—from an imperishable idea of supranational, world-wide character: academic freedom. This is what the university demands and what it is granted. Academic freedom is a privilege which entails the obligation to teach truth, in defiance of anyone outside or inside the university who wishes to curtail it.

The university is a school—but of a very special sort. It is intended not merely as a place for instruction; rather, the student is to participate actively in research and from this experience he is to acquire the intellectual discipline and education which will remain with him throughout his life. Ideally, the student thinks independently, listens critically and is responsible to himself. He has the freedom to learn.

The university is the one place where by concession of state and society a given epoch may cultivate the clearest possible self-awareness. People are allowed to congregate here for the sole purpose of seeking truth. For it is a human right that man must be allowed somewhere to pursue truth unconditionally and for its own sake.

At the same time, however, state and society have an active interest in the university, for it prepares its graduates for those careers in public service which require scientific ability

1

and intellectual training. Few will deny the potential usefulness of the kind of intellectual training which the university
graduate derives from participation in honest research, regardless of subject and specific results. Yet even if such practical utility were open to doubt, man's basic determination
remains unshaken: to seek for truth without limit and at any
price. Without this determination to drive him on he could
never climb to those levels of insight of which he is capable.
Thus, the university is an institution with practical objectives,
but it attains them by an effort of the spirit which at first tran-
scends them only to return to them afterwards with greater
clarity, strength, and calm.

It is impossible to put readily into words what truth is
and how it is acquired. Here, the answers manifest themselves
only indirectly, in the very life of the university, and even then
they are not final. What follows, therefore, is only a provisional attempt to formulate some of these answers.

The university is the corporate realization of man's basic
determination to know. Its most immediate aim is to discover what there is to be known and what becomes of us
through knowledge. This eagerness to know expresses itself
through observation, through methodical thought, and through
self-criticism as a training for objectivity. It is active even
where we confront the very limits of all knowledge and the
special risks and tensions inherent in any intellectual quest.

Oneness and wholeness are of the very essence of man's
will to know. In practice this oneness and wholeness is realized only in specialized fields, yet these very specialties are not
alive except as members of a single body of learning. Integration of the various disciplines joins them into a cosmos
which culminates in the vision of unified science, in theology,
and in philosophy. To be sure, this cosmos includes polarities
which time and again break apart into conflicting and mutually exclusive opposites. The unity of knowledge survives
nonetheless. For despite great diversity in subject and prob-

lem, scholars remain united by a common scientific* outlook.

The university, then, is an institution uniting people professionally dedicated to the quest and transmission of truth in scientific terms.

Because truth is accessible to systematic search, research is the foremost concern of the university. Because the scope of truth is far greater than that of science, the scientist must dedicate himself to truth as a human being, not just as a specialist. Hence, the pursuit of truth at the university demands the serious commitment of the whole man. The university's second concern is teaching, because truth must also be transmitted.

Understanding, moreover, presupposes the intellectual maturity not just of the mind but of the whole man. It therefore follows that instruction and research must aim for more than the transmission of bare facts and skills. They must aim for formation of the whole man, for education in the broadest sense of the term.

To map out the idea of the university means to orient ourselves by an ideal which we can never more than approximate. We shall proceed in three ways.

We shall, first, consider the nature of intellectual life in general, one of whose forms is realized in the university. Next, we shall turn to the responsibilities inherent in the corporate realization of intellectual life at the university. Lastly, we shall consider the concrete foundations of the university and how these affect its functioning.

* The German term *Wissenschaft* covers study in both the sciences and the humanities. Hence, throughout this book, "scientific" must always be understood in both senses at once.

PART I: *The Intellectual Life*

If the university serves science and scholarship and if science and scholarship are meaningful only insofar as they are part of a comprehensive intellectual life, then this intellectual life is the very life blood of the university.

Intellectual life can take many forms apart from that at the university. At the university it is characterized by an institutionalized and orderly collaboration of scholars. Thus, in order to understand the idea of the university and its institutional forms we must say something about the intellectual life in general and about the nature of science and scholarship in particular.

CHAPTER ONE: *The Nature of Science and Scholarship*

Basic Characteristics of Science and Scholarship

Science and scholarship represent a kind of knowledge which is methodical, cogent and *universally valid*. Let us take up each of these three characteristics of scientific knowledge.

First of all, science and scholarship are inseparable from a *sense of method*. The subject I am working with itself determines how I must go about getting results. My method defines the point of view and limits of the material I am working with. The very opposite of scientific thinking is unmethodical guesswork and an uncritical acceptance of ideas on good faith. Even if what is accepted in this way happens to be the result of scientific inquiry, that does not make the uncritical acceptance of ideas any the less unscientific. Such knowledge is in fact a sort of superstitious "science worship." Unless I myself have control over the ideas which I accept, I fall a defenseless victim to those ideas. Knowledge retains its relativity only when we understand the method by which it was attained, when we understand its point of view and its significance. When we do not so qualify "fact" it becomes deceptively absolute.

Secondly, scientific knowledge is *cogent*. The kind of truth which I can understand scientifically is a matter of purely rational evidence. It is right as it stands and requires no additional personal commitment on my part. Conviction is the very opposite of this form of knowledge. Its truth hinges on my personal commitment to it in terms of my own life. That is why Galileo could meaningfully recant before the Inquisition. (After retracting his moving earth hypothesis he is reputed to have said, "But it moves nevertheless."

This is true not to the letter but to the spirit of what took place. Galileo knew that his disavowal could not change the truth.) In Bruno, on the other hand, a willingness to make concessions and retract all nonessential doctrine went hand in hand with a heroic refusal to disavow his most basic philosophical convictions. Their truth, because it was not cogent on a purely theoretical plane, would have been refuted by Bruno's disavowal. Thus, their truth was properly not established until proven in terms of the philosopher's unwavering and enthusiastic endorsement.

Thirdly, scientific findings have *universal validity*. Their cogency can be verified by anyone. Because of this, the dissemination of scientific knowledge is coextensive with the presence of the scientific outlook. Consensus is the mark of universal validity. Therefore scientific truth prevails wherever people think in scientific terms. In philosophy such universal validity is conspicuously absent. For if a given philosophical conviction could command universal acceptance, it would not need my personal commitment to it. Conversely, the relativity of scientific knowledge is connected with its universal acceptance. Research could not progress if its universally cogent findings were valid in an absolute sense.

The Narrower and the Wider Concept of Science

This concept of scientific knowledge, simple though it is, has been slow in evolving and is perpetually threatened. It requires our unending effort in its behalf. Science is not the whole of thought. If it were, the child's earliest attempts at symbolizing would be science. Science, moreover, is not tantamount to arranging concepts in logical sequence. It is not the rational ordering of concepts and phenomena either. Science does not begin until sharp boundaries are drawn within the whole of thought, marking off the scientific form of knowledge from the nonscientific forms.

Science in this narrower and proper sense arose con-
jointly with the extension of knowledge. It began as a science
of discovery: as research.

This research became methodical in a new way. A trial
hypothesis is tested, confirmed or refuted in practice. This is
a battle with the data. The data is not taken for granted but
examined as to its possible implications. We implement our
desire for ever-increasing accuracy by putting our hypothesis
in mathematical language and refining our observations
through better measurements. To make coincidence or disagreement between hypothesis and observation fruitful as criteria we must first define with maximal accuracy the terms of
this agreement or disagreement; i.e. hypothesis and observation itself. Science not only outstripped all previous standards
of universal cogency but clarified its own assumptions in each
case. It is "objective" only in the sense of considering all assumptions tentative and rejecting any that obscure or distort
truth and reality for the sake of a particular bias. Science em-
ploys trial hypotheses which it fully acknowledges as such
and which it tries out for their potential fruitfulness as tools
of discovery.

Only experience can test the truth of scientific assumptions. The success or failure of any hypothesis is due to factors beyond the particular application of the hypothesis but
involves the whole of truth. Is it chance which favors a few
among a multitude of speculations and disregards the rest?
Is it his luck, his unforeseen closeness to reality which directs
the scientist's choice? Is it an unaccountable intuitive power?
In retrospect, the great discoveries always seem to follow
naturally from their underlying principles. Yet in their own
day the full theoretical significance of these discoveries was
never entirely clear.

How were Galileo and Lavoisier able to set in motion
trends of investigation which along with new offshoots continue to be effective to this very day? Thus, for example,

Lavoisier made certain assumptions all of which were made before him, but which he was the first to elevate to the status of permanent and unqualified truths: That which can be dissolved no further is an element. Matter can neither be created nor destroyed. Weight is the reliable index of mass, as all matter is subject to the same force of gravity. Scales had been used before his time. But he was the first to rule out, as a matter of basic principle, any exception or compromise with logical consistency which would interfere with the evidence of his scale readings. Lavoisier's assumptions ran counter to sense evidence. This flagrant discrepancy constituted a standing temptation to abandon these assumptions. What then makes Lavoisier different from a speculative fanatic? Was his achievement due to his intellectual caliber, or just happy coincidence? Neither. The reason his theory succeeded was that scientists were prepared to accept the absolute truth of his presuppositions since they could independently verify his experiments.

Every era has had its self-appointed "custodians of truth" who greet any radical attempt to introduce new premises with a storm of protest. All that such criticism accomplishes is this: that all branches of learning work with hypotheses of only relative validity which do not describe reality itself but only particular aspects of its appearance. Presuppositions have only tentative validity. What few "hits" there are among the countless ineffectual efforts of pure speculation are usually amazingly productive. Hence the genuine scholar and scientist distrusts all pure speculation which cannot furnish proof of past or future fruitfulness.

What characterizes science then, is this: We cannot achieve universally valid and cogent knowledge of reality except within a framework of assumptions which we know to be only relatively valid.

The new science began as a *mathematical* science of nature, motivated by a revolutionary concept, the universal applicability of the scientific method. Even Greek science, with the exception of certain forms of mathematics and of Platonism, lived by the idea of initial perfection and thought of itself as essentially complete. Its universality was based on the conception of a closed finite cosmos. On the other hand, the universality of the "new science" does not reside in an all-inclusive world-system, but in open-minded readiness to subject everything to scientific investigation. True, the form of Greek science survives to the present day. It survives in the average understanding as a distortion of the real meaning of modern science. Modern science is prepared to penetrate ever deeper into the infinite expanse of Being by continuing to build upon previous discovery. It endeavors to search out things hitherto unnoticed, to realize not a cosmos, but the idea of a cosmos of scientific methods and the unity of science in an "open-ended" universe.

Along with the new openness of inquiry there arose a new sense of the richness of reality and of the gaps between the different levels of being—the lifeless, the living, the soul, the mind. People also gained a new systematic awareness of the different categories of understanding. At first the "new" scientists impoverished reality by reducing it to causal, logical and quantitative terms (measuring, counting). In short, they wanted to make the world understandable in terms familiar from the production of artifacts. Gradually, however, the categories of understanding were more clearly defined, thus preventing the confusion of categories without the sacrifice of any already existing ones. Everywhere there was a shift of focus to what is universally valid and cogent.

In achieving clarity about its own methods and limitations the new science necessarily set free that mode of thought from which it differed. For there is a type of thinking which produces insights without universal validity and cogency, yet of fundamental importance to life itself. This type of thinking penetrates to the heart of reality not through analy-

ses but through flashes of insight. Because science is limited
to the cogent and universally valid, scientific research and discovery is limited to the study not of Being itself but of its
appearances. Opposed to this narrower concept of science
there is a broader one. Science can acknowledge this broader
concept as complementary and perhaps even basic to itself,
provided confusions are avoided. The type of thinking which
illumines by flashes of insight is not part of science but has its
own independent roots.

Science in this wider sense includes any clear understanding obtained through rational and conceptual means. Thinking so understood does not provide insights into matters
hitherto unfamiliar, but clarifies what it is I really mean,
want or believe. Science in this broader sense is identical with
the area of lucid self-knowledge.

Then there is a form of thought (speculative philosophy,
for example) which requires our personal commitment in order to achieve the status of truth.

Finally, thought may function as a cipher or code, simultaneously disclosing and concealing reality.

These splendid and life-inspiring efforts of the human
mind are scientific solely by virtue of their clarity and rigor.
They are at the same time more and less than science. They
are more insofar as they are a creative way of thinking, one
that transforms man. They are less than science insofar as
they do not yield any concrete knowledge. It is therefore of
decisive importance to know what is meant by the narrower
concept of science. This is the concept which modern man
has in mind, however vaguely, when he speaks of science. For
it alone concerns itself with cogent, universally valid knowledge and thus does not require my total personal commitment.
Moreover, the very clarity of science throws into bold relief
what is unique and indispensable in the aims, evidence and
procedure of philosophy. For philosophy cannot fully realize

its possibilities except side by side with science, in distinction from science, and in aiming beyond science.

The Limits of Science

Science in the narrower sense is irrevocably limited in the following ways: Scientific knowledge of things is not the knowledge of Being. Scientific knowledge is of the particular. It is directed toward clearly designated objects, not toward Being itself. By the very knowledge which it achieves, science emphatically highlights its philosophic ignorance concerning Being itself.

Scientific knowledge cannot provide life with goals, values or direction. The very clarity of science points to a source other than science for human life as a whole.

Science, moreover, is unable to tell us its essential meaning. Its existence is due to motives whose truth and cogency are themselves beyond scientific demonstration.

The limits of science have always been the source of bitter disappointment when people expected something from science that it was not able to provide. Take the following examples: a man without faith seeking to find in science a substitute for his faith on which to build his life; a man unsatisfied by philosophy seeking an all-embracing universal truth in science; a spiritually shallow person growing aware of his own futility in the course of engaging in the endless reflections imposed by science. In every one of these cases, science begins as an object of blind idolatry and ends up as an object of hatred and contempt. Disenchantment inevitably follows upon these and similar misconceptions. One question remains: What value can science possibly have when its limitations have become so painfully clear?

Science as Utilitarian versus Science
as an End in Itself

Since Bacon and Descartes people have sought to justify science by pointing to its usefulness. Descartes considered the following as decisive motivations for science: its uses for labor-saving devices, for the better fulfillment of human wants, for the improvement of health, for improved efficiency on the political and communal levels, finally even for the invention of a "scientific morality." On closer inspection we see first that all technical applicability has its limits; technology is only one field in the vast realm of human possibility. Secondly, the great fundamental discoveries are manifestly not due to the considerations of their practical utility. Such discoveries were made without any thought to their applicability. They well up from levels of the inquiring mind which we cannot control or predict. Fruitful application in a host of particular inventions is possible only once the theoretical groundwork has been laid. The spirit of research and the pragmatic spirit of invention differ essentially. It would be absurd, to be sure, to contest either the usefulness of science or its right to serve the practical ends of living. These do give meaning to some branches of science. But practical usefulness cannot be the whole or the only meaning of science. This is because the need for certain inventions did not give rise to science (the great discoverers were on the whole not inventors). Invention alone could not keep scientific research alive permanently.

Some people have countered the subordination of science to technology and the improvement of living conditions by solemnly pronouncing science an end in itself.

Indeed, science is an end in itself to the extent that it expresses man's fundamental and primary thirst for knowledge. This thirst for knowledge intrinsically precedes all considerations of usefulness. For knowledge reduced to pragmatic

terms is not the whole of knowledge. Man's fundamental
quest does not stand or fall with any one educational ideal of
history. Here knowledge is valued exclusively from the
standpoint of common standards and forms and for its ability
to shape the whole person according to the accepted ideal.
Plain curiosity, the naïve desire to see the strange and unknown
and to learn about them at second hand in the form of experience and results, comes closer to preserving the primary fresh-
ness of man's quest for knowledge. But curiosity only touches
things without seizing them. Quickly aroused it quickly loses
interest. Before it can become an element of knowledge, curiosity must first be transformed.

Thus transformed it no longer requires justification of any
sort and is correspondingly less able to account for itself.
Man alone among all other beings considers himself human
only so long as he involves himself in the process of knowledge. He alone is willing to face the consequences of this
knowledge. He takes this risk because, regardless of the consequences to his personal existence, truth is his reward. Indeed, we come to know ourselves only insofar as we come to
grips with the world about us, with the various levels and
kinds of knowledge and with the intellectual formulation of
possible lines of thought and action.

Man's primary will to know struggles against the self-
satisfied formalism of empty learning which drugs man into
the illusory calm of fulfillment. It fights against empty intel-
lectualism, against nihilism which has ceased wanting anything
and thus has ceased wanting to know. It battles against me-
diocrity which never takes stock of itself and which confuses
knowledge with the mere learning of facts and "results." The
only satisfaction which man derives from a radical commitment to knowledge is the hope of advancing the frontier of
knowledge to a point beyond which he cannot advance except
by transcending knowledge itself.

The slogan "science an end in itself" was coined to ex-

press man's primary and unconditional thirst for knowledge.
It has been erroneously taken to certify the intrinsic value of
any factual discovery whatsoever, of each and every correct
application of method, extension of knowledge, and scientific
occupation. Chaos ensued. There was the uncounted mass of
arbitrary factual finding, the diffusion of the sciences into a
vast unrelated aggregate; the complacency of specialists ig-
norant of and blind to the larger implications; the triumph of
the "production line" approach to learning, forever losing itself in the endless waste of mere factual correctness. Mecha-
nized and drained of all meaning, intrinsic or human, science
became suspect along with its claim to have intrinsic value.

The motto "science an end in itself" is in ill repute. The
much invoked crisis of science resulted in the disavowal of all
of its meaning. It was claimed that science will serve any
master, that it is a whore; that it leaves the soul empty; that
it is a production line indifferent to the human heart; that, essentially, it spends its time carting rubble back and forth.

These charges do apply to a degenerate pseudo-science,
but not to man's primary quest for knowledge. If for medieval man knowledge culminated in the vision of God; if
Hegel, in all seriousness, spoke of logical thinking as an act of
religious worship; if even the logical positivist acknowledges
the existence of the unknowable, then we too can experience
human fulfillment in truth. More radically than ever before,
men are thinking about what truth is. Modern man remains
intensely alive to the ancient wisdom that nothing except the
discovery of truth gives meaning to our life (even though we
lack final certainty as to what that meaning is and what it implies); that nothing is exempt from our desire for knowledge;
and that, above all, life seeks to base itself upon thought. These
age-old insights, irreducible to psychology and sociology, have
attested man's higher origin.

The only access to these conclusions is by way of science.

It remains to clarify the nature of true science conceived in this way.

The Basic Assumptions of Science

The slogan "science assumes nothing" was meant as a battle cry against restrictions which would have been imposed upon learning in the form of specific unquestionable dogmas. This "battle cry" was justified to the extent that it signified science's refusal to commit itself to preconceived conclusions, to limit the scope of its inquiry, to consider anything as "taboo" or to sidestep certain inevitable conclusions.

In fact, however, there is no such thing as a science without assumptions. What is characteristic of science is that it recognizes and clarifies these assumptions in a spirit of self-criticism. Strictly speaking, science represents a tentative body of thought aware of itself and aware that whatever validity and consistency it has derives from certain specific assumptions.

Thus, science presupposes the validity of the rules of logic. Where the principle of contradiction is denied thinking and knowing are impossible. Thought intrinsically recognizes this principle. Where concepts are allowed to become vague and equivocal, where self-contradiction is not deemed an objection, speech itself has ceased to be meaningful communication. Any statement denying certain logical assumptions must respect them at least for the duration of this very denial. Whoever is unwilling to acknowledge these assumptions is unamenable to argument and can only be left alone like the "irrational plant" to which in Aristotle's phrase he has degraded himself.

We are mistaken, therefore, when we absolutize knowledge. Knowledge is possible only where the laws of logic are respected. Consequently, what is known is not Being per se but those aspects of reality which present themselves in terms of the conditions imposed by our own thinking process.

Moreover, science presupposes its own desirability. It is impossible to defend science on grounds themselves scientific. No science can prove its value to one who denies it. Man's primary craving for knowledge is autonomous. We crave knowledge for its own sake, a passion whose self-affirmation remains the permanent premise of all science.

A further important assumption of science pertains to the choice of subject to be investigated. The scientist selects his problem from among an infinite number of possibilities. Obscure instincts, love and hatred may motivate his choice. In every case it is will, not scientific knowledge, which makes him decide to take up a particular subject.

Lastly, science presupposes that we let ourselves be guided by ideas. It is only through such "schemes of ideas," as Kant called them, that our minds are guided by the encompassing whole around us, even though this encompassing whole cannot itself become an object of cognition and all our conceptual schemes have only auxiliary and provisional significance. Ideas and hypotheses are thus auxiliary constructs which must disappear again for they are inevitably finite and thus inevitably false. Yet without such ideas to guide us there is no unity of focus, no direction, no distinction between trivial and important, basic and superficial, significant and meaningless, wholeness and diffusion. They form the context which motivates our special interests, permits flashes of insight and discovery and lends meaning to pure chance. The unending number of conceptual outlines guiding us, futile as they are each alone, are our only way of relating ourselves to the infinite. Yet these guiding ideas have to come alive in the scholar himself before learning can have any meaning.

All sciences make such assumptions. To these may be added the particular assumptions of particular disciplines. The theologian, for instance, believes in miracles and revelation. These topics are inaccessible and therefore nonexistent to empirical science—so far as scientific explanations are concerned. "Since science disclaims assumptions of a theological kind it requires the believer to admit no less, but also no more than this: granted that a given sequence of events is to be explained without reference to supernatural interference, such being inadmissible as empirical cause, then this sequence must be explained in the manner attempted by science" (Max Weber). Any believer can admit this much without becoming untrue to his faith.

Theological science proceeds differently. Assuming the existence of revelation, theology clarifies the implications and consequences of this faith. It develops special categories to express the inexpressible.

Both explanations, the secular and the theological, operate with assumptions. They are not, strictly speaking, mutually exclusive. Both are forms of thought which work with assumptions and see where and how far they will get with them. Both remain scientific so long as they acknowledge one another and remember in a self-critical spirit that knowability is but a mode of Being within Being, never Being per se.

When we point out that all science proceeds from necessary assumptions it is equally important to make clear what, contrary to widespread belief, we need not assume: that the world is entirely knowable, or that knowledge deals with Being itself; or that knowledge is somehow absolute in the sense of containing or providing nonhypothetical knowledge. The converse is apparent the moment we reflect on the limits of knowledge.

Nor does science presuppose a dogmatic Weltanschauung. Quite the contrary. Science exists only to the extent that such a *Weltanschauung* does not enjoy absolute validity, or, if it does, only if its results can survive the crucial test of unbiased examination, to the extent, in short, that Weltanschauung remains a mere hypothesis.

For decades people have noisily denied (no critical student had ever asserted it) that science can dispense with assumptions. It is useful to point out the dangers attendant upon this one-sided emphasis. All too easily all meaning is drained out of the sciences and concentrated on the premises alone, thus rendering them dogmatic. Well-meaning people, but poor craftsmen, unproductive in the sciences and uninterested in methodical study reject what they do not even know. In place of science they want something entirely different: politics, church, propaganda for various irrational drives. Instead of working hard and devotedly at their subjects and looking at things concretely, they allow themselves to slip into pseudo-philosophical talk, generally about the "whole," the "total picture." The most necessary of all presuppositions for science is a sense of direction. It has often been forgotten that science even so much as needs direction.

Science Needs Direction

Left to itself science loses this sense of direction. For a while it may seem to advance spontaneously, but this is but the lingering momentum of an impulse itself due to a deeper cause. Soon, however, contradictions become apparent which threaten to bring about the collapse of the entire structure. Science as a whole is neither true nor alive without the faith on which it rests.

This can be expressed in another way. Unable to fend for itself science needs direction. Where this direction comes from, and what meaning it imparts to science is decisive for the self-realization of science. Neither utility nor "science as an end in itself" can, so we have seen, constitute the real impulse for scientific activity. Agencies external to science may, to be sure, utilize it as a means to nonscientific ends. But then the full meaning of science remains veiled. If, on the other hand, scientific knowledge becomes its own ultimate aim, then science is meaningless. The direction must come from within, from the very roots of all science—from the unqualified will to

know. In submitting to the guidance of this primary thirst
for knowledge, we are not ultimately led by some goal we
can know or name in advance. We are led by something we
find growing ever keener as we master knowledge—that is
by responsive reason. How is this possible?

Our primary thirst for knowledge is not just a casual interest. It is a compelling necessity for us which forces us on as
if knowledge held the very key to our human self-realization.
No one piece of knowledge can satisfy us; tirelessly we keep on
going, hoping to embrace the very universe through knowledge.

Propelled as it is by our primary thirst for knowledge, this
search is guided by our vision of the oneness of reality. We
strive to know particular data, not in and for themselves, but
as the only way of getting at that oneness. Without reference
to the whole of being science loses its meaning. With it, on
the other hand, even the most specialized branches of science
are meaningful and alive.

This oneness or wholeness of reality is not to be found in
any one place. All I can ever know is a particular instance
among an endless variety of things. Thus, what determines the
actual direction of any inquiry is our ability to perpetuate, yet
continuously to interrelate two elements of thought. One is
our will to know the infinite variety and multitude of reality
which forever eludes us. The other is our actual experience
of the unity underlying this plurality. Still, that experience
of unity cannot be had except as we face up to the fragmentary character of all human knowledge.

In one sense, then, science makes us face the facts pure
and simple. Evermore sharply we realize "this is the way
things are." We begin to understand what the appearances of
things seem to be saying. Science compels us to face the factual appearance of things and forego premature simplification
and wishful thinking. Science disenchants—destroys my rap-
ture at the beauty and harmony of the world. Instead it fills

me with horror at the cacophony, meaninglessness and unaccountable destruction of things.

In a second sense, experiencing my genuine ignorance I grow aware, if indirectly, of the unity transcending and secretly motivating my entire search for knowledge. Only this unity gives life and meaning to my search.

This meaning can no longer be rationally defined because it is beyond knowledge. Since it is unknowable it cannot serve as the presupposition for our choice of scientific objectives and methods. Only after we have committed ourselves to the quest for knowledge can we learn the source and meaning of knowledge.

If I ask myself where all this knowledge is headed for, I can only answer in metaphorical terms. It is as though the world wanted itself to be known; as though it were part of our glorification of God in this world to get to know the world with all our God-given faculties, to rethink as it were the thoughts of God, even if we ourselves can never grasp them except as they are reflected in the universe as we know it.

To the extent that learning is guided by the original impulse to rational inquiry, an impulse at once responsive to yet transcending the world about us, to that extent alone it has meaning and value. Though it is philosophy which provides this guidance, it cannot be expected to produce at will what must be left to mature spontaneously within each thinker by himself.

From all this I can conclude that science is not the firm ground on which I can rest. It is the road along which I travel so that I may grow aware of the transcendence guiding my will to know. I travel this road with all of that restless thirst for knowledge which characterizes our life in the realm of time.

Granting this view of science as a way—not an end—we shall understand that our many frustrations with knowledge are due to a loss of inner guidance. We recognize that loss whenever we allow ourselves to drift, whether from idle curiosity or because science has just become something to keep us busy. These are blind alleys from which we keep returning to heed that inner sense of direction which determines our course of study and research. We have a bad conscience when we give in to mere "industry" to drown our sense of hopelessness. Such "industry" cannot disguise the deadly inertia of meaningless work. Instead we ought to make ourselves receptive to the ideas which guide our work. These ideas stem from the transcendent wholeness motivating our search.

This concept of wholeness which guides our search, however, is not unequivocal. No one is able to grasp it in its fullness or to claim that what he grasps is universally true. No one can claim to be its sole possessor. This guidance becomes effective only in the dialogue between the thinker and the manifold objects of knowledge. It is realized through the continued forward and upward surge of learning at each point in history. It involves trial and risk. This is why science can supply the driving force toward truth and truthfulness in our daily lives.

Science as the Presupposition of Truthfulness

Science unmasks illusions with which I would like to make life more bearable, by which I hope to replace faith or at least to transform faith into certain knowledge. Science disperses half-truths which serve to hide realities I am unable to face. It breaks up the premature constructs which uncritical thinking sets in the place of tireless research. It keeps us from lapsing into deceptive complacency.

Science furnishes a maximal clarity concerning the condition of man in general and of my own person. Science provides the conditions without which I cannot live up to the challenge implicit in my native capacity for knowledge. Fulfilling this task is man's great destiny. It challenges him to show what he can make of himself through knowledge.

Science springs from honesty and produces it. We cannot

be truthful unless we have absorbed a scientific attitude and
mode of thought. It is characteristic for a scientific attitude
always to differentiate between what is known cogently and
what is not known cogently (I want to know what I know and
what I don't know). This knowledge includes the way which
leads to knowledge and the boundaries within which this
knowledge is valid. The scientific attitude is further characterized by readiness to accept any criticism of one's assertions. For the thinking man, for the scientist and philosopher,
in particular, criticism is a necessary condition of life. There
can never be enough of the kind of questioning which compels him to examine his insights. A genuine scientist can profit
even from unjustified criticism. He who avoids being crit-
icized essentially does not want to know.

Once the radical will to know, which forms the basis of
the scientific quest for knowledge, has become existential
reality in the life of a human being, no conditions of time and
place can unmake that fact. For whom does science come to
life?—not for those who lose themselves in the never ending
diversity of harmless facts (which they accept without ever
questioning their possible significance); nor for those who
painfully strain to learn material in order to pass examinations or in order to prepare themselves to practice a given
occupation. Knowledge comes to life for the real scientist.
His extraordinary patience and toil become inflamed with
enthusiasm. Science becomes the principle animating his
whole life. Today as at all times the magic of science can be
experienced by young people for whom the world is challenging. And today too (perhaps even more than ever before) we
experience the burden of science; science endangers both the
naive strength of the non-self-conscious as well as the illusions
requisite for living; what Ibsen called the "life lies." It takes
courage to conceive by questioning, instead of merely learning by rote. The old maxim still applies: *sapere aude!* (Dare
to know!)

Science and Philosophy

We are now in a position to make some coherent statements about the relationship of science and philosophy. These two do not coincide. Nor is philosophy just one science among others. It is, in fact, essentially different in origin, method and meaning. Nevertheless science and philosophy are closely connected.

The relationship of science to philosophy

Science defends itself against the confusions attendant upon its being linked up with philosophy. It fights what it takes to be the fruitless interference of speculative effort. In brief, it develops a characteristic hostility toward philosophy.

Yet science is able to acknowledge its own limits. Since it does not grasp the whole of truth it leaves philosophy free to cultivate its own area of inquiry. It neither endorses nor denies the value of philosophical findings. It does not interfere so long as philosophy itself does not pass judgments upon matters accessible to scientific research. Science keeps close watch on philosophy in order to keep it from advancing unfounded statements and imaginary proofs. Science does this to the advantage of both science and philosophy.

Science stands in need of philosophical direction, but not in the sense that philosophy is used by science itself or furnishes science with its proper objectives. These are precisely the ways in which science and philosophy are not to be related. Rather, philosophy is effective in motivating a genuine will to know. Philosophy also furnishes those ideas from which the scientist derives his vision and which determine his choices by impressing his whole person with the essential importance of knowing. Philosophy pervades science. It guides it without itself being accessible to scientific methods. Thus science pervaded by philosophy is philosophy become concrete. As the sciences grow aware of the implications of their own activity they do in fact consciously philosophize. The kind of benefit the scholar and scientist derive from philosophy is not of a practical sort. In studying philosophy they do, however, grow aware of the total context of their work. Moreover, they acquire new and stronger motivations for research and a heightened awareness of what their scientific activity means.

The relationship of philosophy to science

Philosophy acknowledges science as indispensable to it. Although aware of its difference from science, genuine philosophy acknowledges its bond to science. Philosophy never permits itself to ignore realities accessible to knowledge. Philosophy demands to know whatever is real and cogent. It wants what is real and cogent to become fruitful for its growing self-awareness. Whoever philosophizes is impelled toward the sciences and seeks experience in the scientific method.

Because the scientific attitude guarantees truthfulness, philosophy becomes the champion of science against anti-science. Philosophy considers the preservation of a scientific mode of thought indispensable to the preservation of human dignity. Philosophy recognizes the truth of Mephisto's threat: "Disdain reason and science, the greatest of all human powers, and I have you in my grasp."*

* I have had to keep my remarks on science in the form of assertions. I shall take the liberty of referring my readers to the following passages in my other books:

Philosophie. Berlin; J. Springer, 1932, pp. 85ff. (limits of our world orientation); pp. 149ff. (system of the sciences); pp. 212ff. (positivism and idealism); pp. 318ff. (philosophy and science).

Nietzsche; Einführung in das Verständnis seines Philosophierens. Berlin, Leipzig; W. de Gruyter, 1936. The chapter entitled "Wahrheit," pp. 147ff.

Die Geistige Situation der Zeit. Berlin, Leipzig; W. de Gruyter, 1931, pp. 118ff. (science) and pp. 167ff. (the genuine will to know).

Descartes und die Philosophie. Berlin, Leipzig; W. de Gruyter, 1937, pp. 32ff. (the method), pp. 95ff. (the perversion of the meaning of modern science and its effects).

Existenzphilosophie. Berlin, Leipzig; W. de Gruyter, 1938 (passages from the first lecture, entitled "Philosophie und Wissenschaften," and from the second lecture, entitled "Vernunft").

CHAPTER TWO: *Spirit, Human Existence, Reason*

In our attempt to outline the meaning of science we hit upon something that is more than science: its basis and goal. These define the course and direction of scientific work, yet they are not themselves scientifically demonstrable. They become known only in the light of philosophy. The basis and goal of science are essential. Without them science has no meaning for us. Since our chief consideration here is the idea of the university which is characterized by the spirit of scientific inquiry we must limit ourselves to a few seemingly dogmatic remarks.

Spirit,* human existence, and responsive reason make up the all-inclusive context of our lives. Spirit is the potentiality and power of ideas. Human existence in its fullest sense signifies our serious and unconditional commitment to the search for transcendence. Responsive reason is the mind open to the intrinsic meaning of things.

Spirit lives and moves wherever our striving for clarity is a striving for fullness of insight. Without ideas there is no such insight. Ideas impel us from within and at the same time beckon to us as the goal we can never reach. Ideas unify and systematize study and research by furnishing us with hypothetical constructs, themselves only approximations to the ideas themselves. Spirit is the power of creative intuition; without imagination science remains sterile. Such imagination enables us to see what is essential and real, to understand from within, that which lies below the surface, and to make this available to scientific study.

What I call human existence is the firm commitment that supports our whole intellectual existence. Without such commitment all we experience becomes the play ball of hedonistic

* The German term *Geist* means as much "Mind" as "Spirit."

28

contemplation, irresponsible theorizing, and an empty aestheticism. The meaning of what we do eludes all attempts at formulation. It becomes manifest only in our innermost beliefs. Only the seriousness of our personal resolve can allow ideas to become effective in our lives.

If it is the function of mind to consider only entire contexts and configurations, the function of existence to base our lives upon an absolute commitment, it is the function of reason to keep broadening our horizons. Reason opposes isolation; it seeks coherence. To this end reason requires consistent and correlated, not arbitrary or haphazard, thinking, to bring out contradictions, to integrate every isolated thing and thought. Reason makes us seek the kind of understanding that comes from personal experience. It breaks all barriers, overrides all inhibitions; reason gives credit where credit is due and in this fashion preserves the essence of whatever it contemplates.

Spirit, personal commitment, and responsive reason make us aware of the broader context of achievements and possibilities in our lives. It is this context which gives meaning and vitality to science. This explains the secret whose presence makes itself felt everywhere, that what is decisive in science is not manipulative reason and tangible output alone, but a more subtle factor in addition: this is present in craftsmanship and personality rather than in specific results.

Spirit, human existence and reason are the foundation of the scientific outlook. They are the philosophical elements within science even though they never are explicitly acknowledged. Their presence is felt at the frontiers of science. It is these three which can make the passion for knowledge into a passion for genuine Socratic ignorance. This ignorance is not the conditional kind which recedes as knowledge advances, but it becomes apparent in its full depth precisely as knowledge advances in clarity and scope. Philosophical ignorance accompanies the presence of philosophy in all the sciences.

CHAPTER THREE: *Culture*

Culture is an acquired state. That man is cultured who has been shaped by a given historical ideal. A coherent system of associations, gestures, values, ways of putting things, and abilities have become second nature to him. The Greek conception of culture was physical beauty combined with the continuous achievement of excellence; the Roman's, conduct characterized by self-control and consciousness of duty; the Englishman's, the ideal of the gentleman. These cultural ideals may set their bearers apart from other men in one of four different ways. They may differentiate them according to their social class origin: knight, priest, monk, burgher; they may express the intellectual sphere which sets the tone: man of the world, artist and poet, or scholar; they may express the chief area of competence: training in poetry and sports, scholastic learning and competence, training in language and literature, knowledge of technology and the natural sciences; finally, they may express the institution in which this education was acquired: the Greek gymnasium and place of assembly, the princely court, the French *salon,* or the German university. Common to all these cultural ideals is the feeling for form and self-discipline and the sense that culture must become one's second nature through practice, as if all were inborn rather than acquired.

In contrast to the general education of the whole man, what we call specialized training is only one aspect of education. This is training for a specific occupation requiring specialized knowledge and skills.

Social privilege though not identical with education is one of its consequences. In Hellenistic Egypt it was solely his gymnastic education as a Greek ephebe which qualified an Egyptian for public office. Lists were kept of all those so educated. The passing of examinations qualified the Chinese for the privilege of belonging to the caste of literates and of becoming mandarins. The German is called educated only if he has graduated from one of the higher schools, formerly the Latin school alone. Without graduating from one of these schools he cannot enter a university and qualify himself for certain professions.

At times an entire nation has adopted the cultural ideal of a particular class, thus making it general. In this way, the set and uniform characteristics of the English gentleman or the Frenchman became possible, while in Germany no one class had developed a cultural ideal of sufficient suggestive power. Because of this the German lacks a uniform national culture; as a mere member of his nation he remains barbarian. For the German, culture is always a purely personal matter.

As far as culture originates at the university, it takes the form of scholarly and scientific discipline. This is the function of the scientific outlook and of the particular subjects emphasized.

The scholarly and scientific outlook is more than specialized knowledge and competence. It is the ability to suspend temporarily one's own values for the sake of objective knowledge, to set aside bias and special interests for the sake of an impartial analysis of data. In doing this we not only achieve essentially impartial knowledge, but also our personal bias is put in a new light. Fanaticism and blindness are eliminated. The very experience of our limitation creates the basis for true objectivity. The insoluble problems which we confront and which point beyond themselves for their solution teach us to seek the real answers beyond the data at hand. The scientific outlook stands for more than specific factual knowledge. It involves the transformation of our whole person in accordance with reason.

The scientific method calls for objectivity, for devotion to the task, for careful weighing, searching out of contrary possibilities, self-criticism. It does not permit one to think as one pleases and to forget everything else at the whim of the moment. It is characterized by a skeptical and questioning attitude, by caution when drawing general conclusions, by testing the limits and conditions of our assertions.

Without the continuous exercise of reason in the sciences, education in accordance with a fixed ideal will prove rigid and confining. When education trains us to apply reason to every problem and achieve the flexibility of reason in our life as a whole, then it will truly humanize.

A further characteristic of scientific education derives from the special disciplines to which the scholar has dedicated himself. The educational value of the natural sciences and the liberal arts is very different in character. The "realism" of natural science, on the one hand, and humanism, on the other, seem like two distinct cultural ideals. Both rely on scientific research, the one through familiarity with natural phenomena observed and experimented upon, the other through familiarity with books and the works of man subjected to analysis

The liberal arts study the spirit of man. Understanding here involves a meeting of minds across the centuries. We confine ourselves to what we can understand: the men, the works, the period. Only rarely do we touch upon the geographical, racial, and natural premises of the products of the human mind, which elude explanation. All of our life, however, is permeated by these imponderables, which natural science seeks to understand. In the liberal arts we acknowledge these facts as something we explain as outsiders but do not understand intrinsically.

Scholar and scientist each tend to claim that their own discipline is the only true one. Natural science, with its particular knowledge of that reality with which our entire intellectual being is involved, blocks the tendency to ascribe all to spirit. Conversely, the liberal arts oppose the reduction of spirit to matter and biology, with the knowledge that the human spirit cannot be reduced in this way but that it has its own independent origin.

An educational ideal in which humanism and the realism of the natural sciences are joined to one another for their mutual enlightenment has not been realized so far.

The liberal arts are valuable educationally because they allow a realization of the substance of the human past, a participation in tradition, a knowledge of the breadth of human possibilities. Even where the manner of discovery has been forgotten (this is studied by philology) the result as such retains its importance. To assimilate the myths, images and works of a great past has in itself educational value. The educational value of the natural sciences lies in the training for exact observation. The subject matter itself has educational value to a far lesser degree than that of the liberal arts. In physics and chemistry the results are relatively unimportant, whereas the method through which they were obtained has educational value. The natural scientist who knows nothing except results has an essentially dead and meaningless knowledge. He is abetting a distortion of science into dogma and authority.

What most people take to be all-important, the dogmatic unification of scientific results into a system, is precisely what has least educational value for the natural scientist. An item of knowledge the validity of which I cannot independently verify not only lacks all positive educational value but is in fact destructive. The net effect of these systems always false in principle equals that of myths in former times. The only difference is this, that in place of the mythical world of former times we now have a barren system of abstractions. Thus, an abundantly rich and substantial whole is replaced by one infinitely poor. Then as now a world view is accepted on faith, in this case as revealed by the authority of science. Empty scientific abstractions replace a living visual intimacy with nature.

Such is the predicament of the natural sciences. They accomplish the maximum in scientific precision and neatness, create the utmost clarity covering the assumptions implicit in their own knowledge. They confirm Kant's thesis that science is science only to the extent that it maintains mathematical rigor. Here, too, everything hinges on our understanding the successive steps of investigation, hardly anything on our acceptance of results. The natural sciences, however, include a wider field. Even the realm of the inorganic includes an infinite variety of mineral forms. Yet how much more enigmatic and impenetrable a reality manifests itself in organic life! What Kant has written is still valid today: "It is quite certain that we cannot adequately comprehend much less explain organic life and its internal potentialities according to causal-mechanistic principles. So certain is this that one may boldly assert that it would be absurd if men so much as plan or even hope for another Newton to arise who could explain the growth of even a single blade of grass by natural laws which are not themselves ordered according to some further end."

Today the sciences of organic life are engaged in continuing expansion. The subject matter comes close to having independent educational value. For we have obtained insights into a new world of infinite variety, which broaden, clarify and deepen our native intimacy with nature. Consequently, a substitute-religion founded on a biological world view is not quite as bad as one founded on a world view as the one provided by a mechanistic thought-model. What educational value there is in either depends solely upon the extent to which the knowledge of results is translated into actual observation, contemplation, and assimilation of the world about us. To the extent that this knowledge becomes a dogmatic *Weltan-*

schauung, its educational value diminishes. Thus, even if dogmatizations in one form or another really are unavoidable, an authentic mythology full of wonder and magic would still be preferable educationally to any other.

PART II: *The Objectives of the University*

The university is dedicated to the pursuit of science and scholarship. Research and teaching seek to contribute to intellectual culture as a way in which truth becomes meaningful and manifest.

The task of the university may therefore be distinguished into the three functions of research, the transmission of learning, and education to culture. Each of these when considered in isolation is clearly inseparable from the other two. (Ch. 4)

In order to do the work of the university successfully, there must be communication of thinking men. Scholars must communicate with one another, teachers with their students and the students among themselves. Communication of all with all is necessary—each according to his intellectual level. We shall have to take up the meaning of this communication, the forms it may take and its freedom. Here is the living core of university life. (Ch. 5)

The university achieves its objectives within the framework of an institution. This framework is basic to its very existence and is reflected in its procedural and administrative practices. The institution is simultaneously indispensable and a standing threat to the idea of the university. By definition knowledge aims at unification. Isolated disciplines may come and go. Within the cosmos of learning they nonetheless seek one another. The university is articulated in such a way as to represent the unity of knowledge. (Ch. 7)

CHAPTER FOUR: *Research, Education and Instruction*

The student comes to the university in order to study the arts and sciences and to prepare himself for a profession. Despite the apparent clarity of his task and situation the student is frequently perplexed. Overwhelmed by the sheer mass of what can be learned he wants to know what is of chief importance. Orientation lectures, practice sessions, and syllabi only partially help to overcome his difficulties. In the last analysis he must find his own way in the world of lectures, laboratories and seminars.

But the student expects even more from the university. To be sure, he studies a special field and has in mind a definite profession. Still, the university with its aura of tradition represents to him the unity of all branches of learning. He respects this unity and expects to experience it, and through it to arrive at a well-founded *Weltanschauung*. He wants to arrive at truth, wants to gain a clear view of the world and of people. He wants to encounter wholeness, an infinite cosmic order. Science and learning are essentially of the spirit: they seek relations to the totality of all there is to be known.

Yet even with all this, youth is not satisfied. The young person has a heightened sense of the seriousness of life since he is aware of the weighty decisions still ahead. He feels plastic, full of possibilities. He is aware that what will become of him largely depends upon himself. He feels that his daily life is what counts, every hour, every living impulse. The young person wants to learn either by apprenticing himself to a master, through self-discipline, or through frank discussion among friends similarly motivated.

One's expectations are only seldom fulfilled at a university. The first rush of enthusiasm does not last. Perhaps the student never had been quite clear about what he wanted, what he was doing. At any rate, he becomes disillusioned, confused. He ceases striving and loses himself in blind alleys. He studies for examinations only and judges everything according to what use it will have for examinations. He considers his period of study as a painful transitional period before his professional life can begin. The latter now holds the promise of salvation. He says that he is probably too stupid to grasp the essentials, resigns himself to practicing his specialty. On the other hand, his originally creative enthusiasms may lose their vitality and become a matter of lip service. He becomes lazy in his work, wants to grasp the idea, unity, profundity directly without any disagreeable effort which to his way of thinking grasps only trivia. He thinks that by reading a few good books he is doing scholarly work. He finally perverts true effort to the point where he seeks an edifying frame of mind, rather than scholarship, and mistakes the classroom for the pulpit.

If he is lucky, the individual student makes his own way, a way that leads to development and purpose, guided only by his personal intuition. Ultimately, he who does not know where he is going goes the farthest. Reflection on the overall implications of his proposed work will not directly help any man to get his bearings. But it will help him indirectly by making him aware of possibilities and limitations and thus prevent confusion. The aspiring scholar will reflect on the broader questions of direction, order and aims of his work. For the will to know implies the will to understand clearly what one is doing. Our discussion here aims to assist this quest for intellectual clarity as a way of life, a form of human existence.

Three things are required at a university: professional training, education of the whole man, research. For the university is simultaneously a professional school, a cultural center and a research institute. People have tried to force the university to choose between these three possibilities. They have asked what it is that we really expect the university to do. Since, so they say, it cannot do everything it ought to decide upon one of these three alternatives. It was even suggested that the university as such be dissolved, to be replaced by three special types of school: institutes for professional training, institutes for general education possibly involving a special staff, and research institutes. In the idea of the university, however, these three are indissolubly united. One cannot be cut off from the others without destroying the intellectual substance of the university, and without at the same time crippling itself. All three are factors of a living whole. By isolating them, the spirit of the university perishes.

Research

Within the life of the university teachers and students are driven by a single motive, man's basic quest for knowledge. For every advance in knowledge, however, stubborn, indefatigable work is necessary. This work involves three factors:

(1) Work in its narrower sense consists of learning and practicing, widening one's realm of knowledge and mastering methods. Work is the basis of everything else. Work more than anything stands in need of discipline and order. It is most time-consuming and can be initiated at any time. Only hard work can lay the indispensable foundations, can fashion our tools, and can supply the necessary method through which to express and check any new discovery, as well as the actual verification of what would remain mere conjecture. No one can fail to respect the sheer discipline and endurance of persistent effort. The student should start in on this work immediately as he has learned it in school. "The sooner we realize," says Goethe, "that there is a systematic way, call it craft or call it art, of augmenting our natural endowments, the happier we are." But whoever boasts about his craftsman-like competence and thinks that it suffices to make his contribution valuable is lost in a morass of materials and technique. Sheer

industry is not above resenting enviously and ignobly any genuine intellectual competence with its far broader scope.

(2) If work is not to be just endless drudgery, if there is to be meaning in it, it needs something which cannot be attained through good will alone. Ideas which are not rational but truly intuitive first give impetus to the scientist, invest his discoveries with importance. Ideas grow and move. They cannot be compelled by will alone. They grow, however, only for those people who are steadily at work. "Conjectures" are unpredictable and incalculable. That which alone causes learning to thrive—something unclear, opaque to reason and impossible to manufacture—just this demands devoted care. The man who does intellectual research belongs to that group of men who must "forever think about their subject," who are thoroughly permeated by their work. His is not the compartmentalization of life into work and amusement. One's way of life is a requisite condition for ideas, especially if these are to be taken seriously. Many a man has had a good idea but uncaring has soon forgotten it.

(3) Above and beyond mere industry the scholar and scientist has an intellectual conscience. While he realizes that everywhere he must trust to luck and right instinct, he strives at the same time for conscious and honest control over his creative impulses. Unthinking industry without aims, mere feeling and belief, mere consent and edification which do not in turn impel him to a creativity of his own run equally counter to his conscience. The scholar tries to relate chance and isolated occurrences to a whole. He strives for continuity, resists arbitrary interruption of a line of thought. But he does interrupt it when his conscience compels him to follow up some idea which might lead him further. He then turns to pursue this intensively. He is as distrustful of frequent reorientations as he is of absolute continuity along a single line of thought. Because he strives for the ultimate implications of his ideas and wishes to bring these out in his work, he is little

concerned with what is merely fashionable or current. But he is concerned with the present, with the present moment as the incarnation of eternity. He is able to seclude himself. He knows that no one on the outside can judge whether or not he is proceeding correctly. His intellectual conscience decides for him. No outside advice can lighten the burden of his responsibility.

It is the responsibility of the university to promote intellectual work based on these three elements.

The process of learning deals with definite subject matter. Nothing is exempt from this radical quest for knowledge. Whatever exists in the world should be brought into the scope of the university so as to become object for study. Knowledge cannot be created exclusively by the mind. Only the mathematician and the logician are self-contained in this sense and need not go beyond everyday experience. The student at all times requires material for empirical observation. Because the university realizes this, it furnishes him with additional aids, such as collections, libraries and clinics. Materials for study and research or pictures of them, apparatus and experimental equipment are also made available.

Yet inanimate objects alone do not make up all that there is to be known. Mind is intrinsically alive. A given historical period and civilization can achieve genuine self-awareness. It does so when its thinking members stand in a relationship of "give and take" with their own time, when they associate with intellectually productive people. The university exists against the undefinable background of an intellectual atmosphere, a human "give and take" that cannot be induced by an act of will or organization, but either is or is not there. Groups and personal relationships of an incalculable sort are formed. The university is impoverished if this human-intellectual life-blood ceases to pulse through its veins, or if only pedants and philistines continue to concern themselves with living material alien to them as human beings. It is impoverished if there is only philology, no philosophy, only technology, but no theory, endless facts but no ideas.

The always limited world of the university is broadened by travel, by admitting visiting scholars, by broad and personally deep relationships, by foreign connections, or if the university contributes its personnel to some practical tasks which others like doctors serve on a permanent basis. All such practical activity may strengthen the idea of the university, provided it can be shared, turned into ideas, and evoke a response in the community of scholars.

If research is to be the task of the university then this task is realizable at the university only in the face of many conflicting obligations. Some have therefore concluded that it would be better to have institutes for pure research alone, unburdened by any other duties. Such research institutes have in fact been organized and turned out good work. Yet fundamentally they remain offshoots of the university. In the long run they will flourish only in association with the university. They are dependent on the university for their supply of new talent. Moreover, research in itself depends on access to the whole of knowledge, and the opportunity of exchange with all sorts of specialists. Where research institutes are not tied to special places by the nature of their research, they do well to locate in university towns. For a certain time a specialized project can have astounding success, especially in the natural sciences. But the meaning and creative perpetuation of research can only be preserved if it maintains a lively exchange with the whole of knowledge. The individual scientist or scholar may profit from spending a certain length of time, or even the remainder of his life, at a research institute, relieved from the other duties of a university. Yet what he has achieved was accomplished in living exchange with the scholarly community to which he might someday return. Moreover, teaching itself is often—even most of the time—stimulating to research.

Above all, teaching vitally needs the substance which only research can give it. Hence the combination of research and teaching is the lofty and inalienable basic principle of the university. This combination is sound not because it is an economy measure, nor because this combination alone financially enables the scientist or scholar to do his research, but because ideally the best research worker is also the best and only teacher. The research worker may be pedagogically inept, that is, he may be inept in transmitting bare facts. Yet he alone can bring the student into contact with the real process of discovery, hence with the spirit of science rather than with dead results which can be committed to memory. He is the spirit of scientific inquiry come to life; in communication with him one can see knowledge as it genuinely exists. He awakens similar impulses in his students. He directs his students to the source of knowledge. Only he who himself does research can really teach. Others only pass on a set of pedagogically arranged facts. The university is not a high school but a higher institution of learning.

The university has professional schools preparing its graduates for jobs that can only be filled by people with a basically scientific outlook. This requires a familiarity with research and method, as distinct from specialized training in the narrower sense. The best preparation for these special professions is not memorization of a closed body of knowledge but training and development of the faculties for scholarly and scientific thinking. This alone can lay the foundation for further intellectual and scientific training throughout life. The university can only lay the basis for professional training; practice alone brings mastery. The university should provide the best possible conditions for this eventual growth through practice.

The young person must learn how to ask questions. He must study something systematically, get to the bottom of it. He need not, however, carry the sum total of factual knowledge about in his head. Wherever this is the case, it is of no lasting value. After examinations, one quickly forgets. The decisive factor after this is not the body of fact learned, but one's judgment. What matters then is not factual knowledge by itself but the ability and initiative to go out and get the facts on one's own, to think about them effectively, to know what questions to ask. Not memorizing facts but contact with living research imparts this ability. Technical detail, outlines and the like are not excluded but are simply left to textbook study. A bare fifty years ago people used to say that "an institution of higher learning is not a high school." It is certainly a good idea to cover in one's theoretical study as many of the practically useful materials as is possible. But the most important factors even so remain: an active intellect, the ability to grasp problems and to pose questions, the mastery of method.

By its very name the university is a "universe."* Discovery and research constitute an indivisible whole—departmentalization notwithstanding. The university deteriorates if it becomes an aggregate of specialized schools alongside of which it tolerates the so-called "general education" as mere window dressing and vague talk in generalities. Scholarship depends on a relation to the whole. Individual disciplines are meaningless apart from their relation to the whole of knowledge. Therefore it is the intention of the university to impart to its students a sense of the unity both of his own particular field of study and of all knowledge. The whole business of schooling, the mastery of routine and of a body of facts, becomes harmful if it loses this sense of relatedness to the ideal of learning or actually prevents the student from living up to this ideal.

The university, then, must provide the professions with a twofold foundation. It must instill a growing lifelong commitment to the scientific outlook as well as to the search for

* In origin this meant a "universe" of teacher and student, but it has long since shifted its meaning to the one indicated above.

the unity of knowledge. These two are requisite for all intellectual professions, which are the professions involving more than the routine practice of specialized technique. The doctor, the teacher, the administrator, the judge, the clergyman, the architect, are each in his own way professionally concerned with man as a whole, and the conditions of human life as a whole. Preparation for these professions is unthinking and inhuman if it fails to relate us to the whole and to develop our perceptiveness, to show the wide scope of knowledge or to make us think philosophically. Deficiencies in professional routine which are bound to exist at the time when the degree is conferred can be eliminated with practice. Basic deficiencies in scholarly and scientific training are irremediable.

Everyone engaged in an intellectual profession is bound to think in scholarly terms. The true scholar or scientist, however, is he who can persist in the effort of protracted thinking without losing sight of the whole. Hence the best way of imparting practical scientific training is to encourage the habit of research.

To address oneself to the whole is what is called the "philosophical" point of view. All science is "philosophical" in this sense, so long as it does not neglect the end for the means, and so lose itself and its ideal in a concern for cataloguing words and facts, for apparatus, collections, techniques, or isolated phenomena. According to Kant it is the dignity, the absolute value of philosophy which lends value to all other branches of knowledge. This does not mean that everyone should study philosophy. Many a man has evinced his philosophical impulse not only in his novel way of posing questions but in his very attacks upon "philosophy in general." Yet the philosophy that matters is the one at work within science and human life itself, as against the mere vocabulary and jargon of philosophy, which is usually what the detractors of philosophy mean to attack. What matters is the philosophical impulse from which research proceeds, the idea which gives research direction, and the meaning which gives it value and ends of its own. That type of philosophical thought has value which can shape and motivate the scientist and scholar, that philosophy, in short, which permeates the whole of the university. The existence of special chairs for philosophy and of a special department for philosophy, where philosophy can flourish without apparent contact with the whole, is justifiable only on purely administrative and pedagogical grounds.

Education as Formation of the Mind

Formal education, like tradition, generally tends to be dependent upon particular forms of social organization. The changes in educational outlook parallel the changes which a nation undergoes in the course of its history. The unifying factor in education reflects the dominance in each case of a given social body, e.g., church, class, nation. Education could be described as the manner by which these social bodies perpetuate themselves from generation to generation. Hence education becomes transformed when there are social revolutions. Moreover, attempts at social innovations turn to pedagogical questions first. Because of this, considerations of the significance and methods of education inevitably include the larger question of state and society. Blueprints for the good society such as Plato's *Republic* treat political and educational organization as co-extensive. Education prepares each individual to be a member of society and, conversely, society is the means of the individual's education.

Let us consider some aspects of education from the point of view of the historical changes to which they have been subject. The social need of the times determines what will be included in the curriculum. Theological knowledge is required in preparation for the ministry; training in the skills of using language, for a humanistic education. For the education

of the Greek gentleman a knowledge of myth and legend is
required. Today, the importance of sociology, economics,
technology, natural science and geography is stressed. Education changes with cultural ideals. The way schools are organized mirrors the social structure. In the past diverse types
of educational systems have been attempted such as schools
for the several estates, academies for the nobility and private
instruction for aristocrats and patricians. All democracies demand common public education because nothing makes people so much alike as the same education.

Apart from sociological and historical considerations, we
can distinguish three basic forms of education:

(1) Scholastic instruction. This type of education is limited to the mere "transmission" of the tradition. The teacher
only reproduces, he is not himself active in original research.
All knowledge has been systematized. Certain authors and
books are considered authoritative. The role of the teacher is
an impersonal one; he is a representative who may be replaced
by anyone else who is qualified. All material is reduced to for-
mulae. The medieval teacher dictated a text to his students
and commented upon it. The availability of textbooks has
made dictating superfluous. But the underlying idea of medieval education is by no means dead today. The student subordinates himself to some system of thought which shelters
him yet without thereby subordinating him to any one personality. Knowledge is frozen for all time into an orderly
world picture. Here the student is interested only in what is
fixed and permanent, wants to assimilate results, and like the
pupil in Goethe's *Faust* wants to take home results in "black
and white." The scholastic approach continues to be indispensable to Western rationalism.

(2) Apprenticeship. Of chief importance here is not
an impersonal tradition, but a personality felt to be unique.
The reverence and love rendered to the master's person have
something of worship in them. The distance between master

and pupil derives not merely from a quantitative difference (of two generations), but in addition, from an inherent, qualitative one. The person of the master exerts an authority with a marvelous power. A wide variety of motives comes into play here. There is the need to subordinate oneself, the desire to avoid responsibility, the relief experiencd through association with greatness, coupled with the enhancement of one's sense of self-importance and the need for a discipline sterner than any we can impose on ourselves.

(3) In Socratic education, the teacher and his student ought to stand on the same level. Both are meant to be free. No hard and fast educational system exists here, rather endless questioning and ultimate ignorance in the face of the absolute. Personal responsibility is carried to its utmost and is nowhere alleviated. Education is a "midwifery," in which the student is helped to give birth to his abilities and powers. He is awakened to an awareness of his own capacities, he is not compelled from without. What counts is not the accident of empirical individuality but our true self which emerges in the process of self-realization. The Socratic teacher resists his students' urge to make him their authority and master. Herein lies the greatest temptation for students. He turns them away from himself and back onto themselves; he hides in paradoxes, makes himself inaccessible. The intimate relationship between student and teacher here is not one of submission, but of a contest for truth. The teacher knows that he is only human, demands that his students differentiate between human and divine.

In all three types of education respect is a dominant factor. In scholastic education respect focuses on a tradition visible in the very hierarchy of social structure. In apprenticeship-training respect focuses on the personality of the master; in Socratic education, on the transcendent status of mind which imposes on human life the burden of straddling two worlds.

Respect is indispensable to education. Without it, industriousness at best remains. Respect is the very substance of all education. Man's humanity requires his realization of the absolute. Without it all would be meaningless.

Within the world this absolute can be reflected on three levels: on the corporate level, such as the social group for which one is being prepared, the state, or an institutionalized form or religion; on an individual level; or on both levels simultaneously.

To the extent that its substance becomes problematic, education becomes rigid. Respect is artificially maintained through deliberate secrecy exercised by those in authority. It is maintained also by the demand of blind obedience to a personal authority, and by awakening man's desire for submission. Mere "fulfillment of duty" becomes a substitute for work in behalf of what is essential in education. Instead of striving for one's best achievement, people will seek to gratify their ambitious vanity for recognition and status. The memorization of supposedly useful data replaces the transformation of the entire man by his education. Instead of affirming a given educational ideal with their whole persons such people are only interested in acquiring quickly-to-be-forgotten facts for an examination which supposedly stamps them as educated.

All formal education is free to choose one of these three methods of education above discussed. But it presupposes the value of the educational substance communicated. Without faith in this value no real education can exist, only pedagogical technique.

Once the substance of education has become problematic, the faith in it wavering, the question as to what are the aims of education poses itself. It is a hopeless undertaking, however, to seek such ideals in a manner that ignores the actual historical situation and our own real aims, if, in short, one seeks these ideals in isolation from our own lives. This is the reason why educational slogans such as the following don't amount to much: development of special aptitudes, moral improvement, broadening one's frame of reference, character building, national pride, strength and independence, ability to express oneself, development of the personality, creation of a unifying sense of common cultural tradition, etc.

Education at a university is Socratic by its very nature. It is not the whole of one's education, nor is it like the instruction one receives in high school. University students are adults, not children. They are mature, have full responsibility for themselves. Professors do not give them assignments or personal guidance. Freedom, the all-important factor, is irreconcilable with even so impressive a training as that which has been traditionally identified with the monastic orders and military academies. This type of submission to rigid training and leadership keeps the individual from experiencing a genuine will to know. It blocks the development of human independence that admits no other source or tie than God Himself.

University education is a formative process aiming at a meaningful freedom. It takes place through participation in the university's intellectual life.

Education is not a task to be pursued in isolation. This is why, next to the principle that research and teaching are indivisible, we have a second principle which states that research and teaching are in fact inseparable from the educational process as a whole. Research and professional schooling have an educative effect precisely because they do not just transmit facts and knowledge, but awaken ideas of unity and develop a scientific attitude. To be sure, this development of active intelligence is still less than the training of the whole man. That training involves more. Nevertheless, university education is an integral component of it.

A university so conceived educates in a way which is neither indefinable nor yet definitive. It educates by involving the rational and philosophic impulse, so decisive for the whole man, in its unbounded commitment to the spirit of inquiry and clarification. To the extent that it succeeds in involving the whole man, it enhances his proper humanity, what the Romans termed man's *Humanitas:* the listening to arguments, understanding, the ability to think along with the viewpoints of others, honesty, discipline and consistency. But this type of personality is a spontaneous by-product, not a conscious goal. If education is set up toward this end in isolation from scholarship, what is lost is precisely the intellectual development aimed for. Do we want a thin "humanistic" education which instead of philological, methodical schooling teaches results, offers beautiful objects to be observed, enjoyed and talked about? Do we desire an educational process which reaches deeply into the soul, which directs itself toward religious needs? The university is not a church, no religious order, no mystery, nor is it a place for prophets and apostles. Its principle is to furnish all tools and offer all possibilities in the province of the intellect, to direct the individual to the frontiers, to refer the learner back to himself for all his decisions, to his own sense of responsibility. This sense of responsibility has become awakened through his learning and is brought through it to the highest possible level and the clearest awareness. The university demands a ruthless will to know. Since learning and personal initiative go hand in hand, the university aims for the broadest possible development of independence and personal responsibility. Within its sphere, it respects no authority other than truth in its infinite variety, the truth which all are seeking and yet no one can claim to possess in final and complete form.

The idea of the university derives its educational force from the primary human will to know. It gives the educated man both sureness of purpose and at the same time great humility. Insight alone cannot decide the purpose or ultimate goal of existence. One clear and ultimate purpose is this at any rate: the world wants to be understood. Research belongs to the university not only because it is the basis of training for the professions, but because the university itself exists for research, fulfills its meaning through research. The student is the scholar and scientist-to-be. He will remain philosophically and intellectually oriented for the duration of his life, if he allows himself to grow along with his thinking, even where his way of shaping reality is practical rather than theoretical, a way no less productive than scientific and scholarly achievement measured in terms of published output.

To live freely in the world of ideas is on first inspection fraught with danger for the student. He is thrown back upon his own resources since such a mode of life thrives only on one's own responsibility. From the freedom of teaching springs the freedom of learning. No authority, no rules and regulations, no supervision of studies such as are found in high schools must be allowed to hamper the university student. He is free to "go to the dogs." It has often been said that you have to risk your young men if you want to get a generation of men. There is a place certainly for scholastic instruction, for learning in its narrower sense, and for practice in methods. But the student is free to choose how extensively he wants to participate in this instruction, and when he can get on with books alone, without benefit of teachers.

Ideally the relation between professor and student involves a Socratic equality of status with a mutual stress on standard, not on authority. Intellectual excellence, not mediocrity, sets the tone. We live and work together under the common obligation of calling one another to the highest of standards in thought and performance. Our enemies are smug self-satisfaction and a Philistine attitude. We have a basic desire to be near those whom we admire. Love for the great man, whose very existence makes the greatest demands on us, lends us wings. Still the relation remains Socratic. Nobody becomes authority. The grain of sand remains free and independent next to the cliff. For even the grain of sand is substance. The recognition of an intellectual aristocracy implies making demands upon oneself only, never entitles one to feel superior or make demands upon others. Two things fundamentally unite all members of the university, whether teachers or students; a common calling to exert themselves as if for the very highest attainment, and at the same time, the constant pressure to live up to that calling and prove themselves. It is best in this connection not to indulge in extensive self-analysis, yet on the other hand not to demand outside recognition.

It has been said that students should become leaders of their people. Some have even conceived the strange notion of a school for future leaders. Such notions violate the idea of the university. Leaders come from all classes and occupations. Expert knowledge is attainable not only at a university. Academic training has no monopoly on expert knowledge. It is all well and good to demand "intellectuality" of a leader. In reality, however, leaders are often made of very different stuff. The world is no Platonic Republic, ruled by philosophers. Will to power, resoluteness, deliberation, an eye for the realities of the moment, practical experience and success, as well as special traits of character, are the important qualities. Leaders may well come from academic circles. But generally the type of person found in academic professions is not a leader type. The clergyman, the doctor, the teacher, is certainly a "leader" in a limited sense, either because of his formal authority (which has nothing to do with the idea of the university), as long as this is recognized in the society in which he lives; or he may be a "leader" by virtue of his humanity and spirituality, which manifest themselves in his individual personality. These are again and again put to question, and are never a matter of personal claim. Or he may be a leader because of his expert knowledge, which proves itself useful in his specialty.

Instruction

The mechanics of instruction involve lectures, seminars and laboratories in small private groups, and discussions between two people.

Lectures have held pre-eminence in teaching for ages. They present the materials to be learned in such a way that the listener can visualize how and for what reasons they were collected. Bare facts can be gathered from books. In lectures the listener takes notes and is compelled to think about the lecture. He prepares himself for lectures by doing experiments, studying books, and extending his knowledge.

One cannot establish a standard for good lectures. If they are good they have a special quality which cannot be imitated. Their intended meaning, differing widely with the personality of the lecturer, is valuable in each case. There are lectures which aim to instruct and personally involve the listener, which seek to hold him intellectually; and there are lectures where the speaker, totally oblivious to his audience, engages in a monologue about research in progress, yet even so manages to impart a sense of genuine participation in genuine research. Lectures which aim to sum up an entire subject are in a class by themselves. They are indispensable, for they awaken the impulse to envisage the whole, provided thorough work on the details is being pushed at the same time. Such lectures should be given only by the most mature professors drawing upon the sum total of their life's work. There should therefore be general lectures by the most outstanding professors on each of the basic subjects treated as wholes.

Fundamental disciplines are those whose specific content has universal significance. As against auxiliary subjects and special techniques, their every detail is not an end in itself, but symbolizes the entire cognitive process. Disciplines whose specialized details succeed in mirroring the whole are by that token universal in character. There are textbooks which manage to convey the universality implicit in such disciplines. The manner in which a given discipline investigates its materials reveals the extent to which it is a fundamental discipline.

In the past decades lectures have been subject to much criticism. They are said to be a one-sided affair which encourages a passive attitude on the part of the listener, that any sign as to whether the listener has understood and assimilated the lecture is lacking, that the subject of the lecture is usually better stated in books and can be learned more quickly from these. These objections apply to poor lectures which repeat a dead body of knowledge identically from year to year, or to lectures which are little more than an easy informal flow of talk. Lectures are of value when they become a genuine part of a professor's life work, when they are prepared with care and at the same time inimitably reflect contemporary intellectual life.

Such lectures belong to what is irreplacable in tradition. The memory of outstanding scholars lecturing accompanies one throughout life. The printed lecture, perhaps even taken down word for word is only a pale residue. True, what is of value in the lecture, its content, still communicates in printed form. But the lecturer himself presents this content in such a way as to suggest the total context which motivates his scholarship. Through his tone, his gestures, the real presence of his thinking the lecturer can unconsciously convey the "feel" of the subject. No doubt this can only be conveyed by the spoken word and only in a lecture—not in conversation or discussion. The lecture situation evokes something from the teacher which would remain hidden without it. There is nothing artificial about his thinking, his seriousness, his questioning, his perplexity. He allows us to take part in his innermost intellectual being. This great value is lost the moment it becomes contrived. Right away the result is affectation, rhetoric, pathos, artificial formulas, effects, demagoguery, shamelessness. Hence there are no rules for the preparation of a good lecture. One needs to do no more than to take the matter seriously: to consider the lecture a high point in one's professional responsibility and achievement, finally to renounce all artificiality. In the century and a half of important lectures from Kant to Max Weber it has become evident that even if the speaker falters and makes mistakes in his speech, if his sentences are grammatically incomplete or wrong, if his voice is not effective—none of these things is able to destroy the profound effect of the lecture if its intellectual substance is communicated. Lecture notes convey no more than a weak reflection of actual lectures. Yet even in the absence of personal recollection our imagining what they must have been like can be a challenge to us.

In seminars and laboratory work methods are mastered through practical contact with materials, apparatus and concepts which are studied by concrete example. By his own initiative the student may extend his understanding of these matters. Mastery of techniques occupies the greater amount of effort. We shall not take up the methods of teaching appropriate to different fields and their different technical facilities. Many fields have at their disposal a firm pedagogical tradition to serve as skeleton, not as substitute for instruction.

These seminars and laboratories are designed to acquaint us directly with the subject matter and the elements of learning. They differ basically from courses which merely transmit information, courses which make up for the lack of intellectual initiative on the part of students unable to do better and more rapid work on their own. For in every detail the whole is always implicitly and indirectly present. Textbook knowledge is only incidentally referred to and briefly reviewed in class so as to make the student aware where he has to fill in gaps on his own. The essential factor is to train one's perceptions through personal collaboration on the frontiers of knowledge. The kind of work which best motivates independent study is that which, presupposing general text-book knowledge, deals with a particular problem and goes straight to the heart of the matter. Textbooks by themselves are tiresome. Conversely, to chain oneself to a single object makes one narrow. Each gives life to the other.

Finally, education may take the form of discussion. Questions of basic importance are brought up in small groups, all members of which participate actively. This, in turn, will induce some of the participants to conclude the discussion alone with the teacher in a serious and lively give and take. Here student and teacher meet one another on the same level, as is the ideal. Together they will strive to formulate the problem with such clarity and precision as will awaken impulses in each by himself to make solid, personal contributions later on.

Teaching at the university must not be allowed to "get into a rut." Wherever teaching is intellectually alive it cannot help taking personal form: paradoxically only when the professor has a truly objective approach to ideas does his teaching have genuine individuality. Digressions which are simultaneously objective and personal combine with the special needs of the moment to keep teaching fresh and lively.

Teaching is one thing when it addresses itself to the average student, quite another when it addresses itself to a gifted few. The basic difference between high school and university is that in high schools the teacher must teach all the students entrusted to him. In the university, however, he has no such obligation. University education is meant for a number of selected people who are filled with a very special intellectual zeal and have sufficient mental equipment to do the work. In effect, the people who attend the university are an average group of people who have been able to acquire the necessary preparation. The weeding-out process is therefore up to the university.

The prospective student should have the following quali-

ties: a desire for objectivity and an irrepressible self-sacrific-
ing drive to intellectual attainment. These qualities cannot be
objectively detected ahead of time. Only a minority of people possess these qualities, which in addition, are distributed
in a wholly unpredictable way. They can be cultivated and
made effective only indirectly. Yet it is to this minority
that the university must direct itself if it is to live up to its
own ideal standards. The true student can be relied on to
make his way amid the difficulties and mistakes inevitable
and necessary for intellectual growth, unperplexed by the
mass of courses offered. Selectivity and discipline guide his
studies. We must be prepared to accept, perhaps even welcome, the fact that the rest, at a loss for guidance, will learn
next to nothing. Artificial guides such as the syllabi, curricular
and other technical devices which convert the university into a
high school, are in conflict with the ideal of the university.
They have resulted from adapting the university to the needs
of the average student, on the grounds that the great mass of
students should be made to learn enough at least to pass the
examinations. This line of reasoning, appropriate enough to
the high school, is detrimental to the university, where the
students are adults, even considering no more than their ages.

Nonetheless, university instruction cannot center around
the handful of superlative students. Rohde, the historian of
Greek religion, thought that out of one hundred students
ninety-nine do not understand the teacher and the one hun-
dredth does not need him. If true, that would be disheparten-
ing. University education addresses itself not to the few geniuses or to the mediocre average, but to that minority who
while capable of growth and of initiative, nevertheless stand
in need of instruction.

Some instruction geared to the abilities of the less gifted
and lazy students who are the average is probably indispensable. By and large, however, university education is different. Lectures and seminars which are slightly over the

student's head and so spur him on to increased effort are better than full comprehension purchased at the price of oversimplification. Independent reading and study in laboratories, collections and traveling must complement formal classroom work from the very start. Where instruction is geared to the pace of the brightest among the promising minority already mentioned the mediocre majority of students will have to exert themselves. All are working under a standard which no one entirely satisfies. Respect for the intellectually first-rate must provide all with an incentive to exert themselves to the utmost of their abilities.

Lectures follow one another according to some general order and plan. The sequence in which the beginner hears them is not unimportant. Hence compulsory study plans have come into being. In this way, however, university study ends up being strait-jacketed. The university is turned into a high school in order to achieve a satisfactory average with statistical certainty. This leads to the destruction of the university. As you stifle the student's freedom to learn as he sees fit you stifle the life of the mind. The life of the mind is never more than a chance achievement amid a sea of failure and frustration. It is always something over and above average performance. Both student and teacher are unhappy when chained to curricula and syllabi, to tests and mediocre standards. An atmosphere of uninspired and uninspiring common sense may well produce satisfactory mastery of technical "know how" and testable factual information. Such an atmosphere, however, stifles genuine understanding and the spirit of adventure in research.

CHAPTER FIVE: *Communication*

The university unites people committed to scholarly or scientific learning and the intellectual life. The original sense of *universitas*—a community of teachers and students—is just as important as the unity of all studies. The idea of the university requires the open mind, the readiness to relate oneself to things with the aim of getting at a picture of the whole in terms of one's special discipline. The ideal requires that there be communication, not only on an interdisciplinary but also on an interpersonal level. The university, therefore, should enable scholars to enter into direct discussion and exchange with fellow scholars and students. According to the ideal, this communication must be of the Socratic type, posing questions so that men may achieve clarity about themselves and about each other. An atmosphere of communication based on a community of thinking creates the proper conditions for scholarly and scientific work, although such work is ultimately always solitary.

Intellectually fruitful communication may take the form of friendship between two people, of youth organizations, of love and marriage. There is no need to dwell on the intellectual importance of friendships such as of the brothers Grimm, or Schiller and Goethe, of youth groups such as the original German student fraternity, or of marriages such as that of the Schellings, the J. Stuart Mills, and the Brownings.

The university is the place where truth is sought unconditionally in all its forms. All forms of research must serve truth. The radical character of this commitment creates strong intellectual tensions at the university. They are the very condition of progress. The tensions which flare up into intellectual battles are meaningful by virtue of the common ground which emerges in the course of intellectual dispute. True scholars, even in the heat of controversy, remain firmly united with one another.

They can successfully communicate with one another because their search for truth at the university does not carry with it practical responsibilities. All the university recognizes is responsibility to truth. This struggle for truth must not be confused with a struggle for economic existence. It occurs on the level of disinterested investigation.

Indirect responsibility, for the consequences of one's ideas, for their practical application, is great whether they be true or false or both. What consequences ideas may have cannot be predicted beforehand. The knowledge that such unforeseeable consequences exist, however, makes the responsible thinker cautious. Hegel said, "Theoretical work accomplishes more than practical work. Once the realm of concepts is revolutionized, reality cannot hold out against it." Nietzsche saw this responsibility and shuddered. It is he who threw into the world every idea in its most radical and destructive form. He was intoxicated, yet horrified, by the magic of extremes; he shouted without communicating into the hollowness of his time.

Two things increase the quality of communication. One is the absence of economic considerations and the encouragement this gives to unrestricted experimentation. Another is the responsibility of thought itself, which flourishes much better in an atmosphere of communication than as solitary thought which meets no resistance.

The effectiveness of intellectual formulations and ideas is grounded in truth. Communication is itself a function of the search for truth. It tests truth by testing its effects. Intellectual exchange makes the university the place where people meet who have committed their lives to the search for truth. For the university must not be confused with the sort of school where intellectual spontaneity is rigidly channeled along curricular and pedagogical lines.

For this reason the manner in which communication takes place at a university is the intellectual responsibility of all of its members. The intellectual life at a university declines when its members shut themselves cautiously off from one another, when communication changes into mere sociability, when substantial relationships become obscured by convention. Conscious reflection upon the nature of communication can make such communication possible.

Debate and Discussion

In the sphere of scholarship communication is maintained through discussion. We tell each other what we have found out, but the genuine process of communication begins when our statements are questioned. This takes the form of controversy on highly specialized points. Such controversy becomes philosophical only as it approaches the ultimate issues. Controversy may take either of two forms—debate or discussion.

In logical debate certain set principles are assumed. From these we formally deduce certain conclusions. The opponent is defeated by appeal to the law of contradiction and with the help of countless tricks which the art of logical argumentation has developed since antiquity. One person wins. The mood of the debate is characterized throughout by the desire to vanquish one's opponent. This kind of power-contest—whose consequences can be very useful for formal clarity, even if they do not at all serve the cause of intellectual wholeness—invariably leads to a final break-off of communication in accordance with the principle *contra principia negantem non est disputandum* (You must not argue against someone who denies the very principles of argument).

In a discussion which is meant to serve genuine communication there are no set principles and standpoints firmly maintained until victory. The premises assumed by both parties have yet to be discovered. Both parties seek to clarify their real meaning. Every principle discovered serves as a point of departure for new discussion provided that nothing of what has gone before remains unclear. Each points out the assumptions implicitly made by his partner so that a common ground gradually emerges in the discussion. There is no end. Nobody wins. Those who seem to be "in the right" grow suspicious of their own rightness. Any conclusions reached serve only as stepping-stones.

Real unrestricted discussion is only possible between two people alone. Even a third person is a disturbing factor, easily changing the discussion into a debate, awakening the power instinct. We can, however, discuss to advantage in larger circles. Here we can lay the groundwork for a subsequent and more thorough discussion between two people. Here we can also point out perspectives and positions. Different opinions rapidly succeed one another without any attempt at the kind of stringent discussion which thrives only in rapid private exchange. No conclusions are sought. Thus, there are specific rules for discussion among a number of people: one must not repeat oneself, nor insist on the "correctness" of one's views by repetition. One must not seek to have the last word, but be content to have one's say and then listen to others.

The Formation of "Schools of Thought" as an Instance of Intellectual Cooperation

Every scholarly or scientific accomplishment is ultimately an individual accomplishment. It is personal achievement. It can however be increased through the cooperation of many. Cooperation grows out of communication. When both of these factors are present, motivation, clarity, incentive, reach their highest point; one person's ideas awaken those of another; the ball is tossed back and forth.

Cooperative research is to be distinguished from collective work, which can be described as intellectual industrializa-tion. Something is produced only because the head of the project so directs workers whom he calls associates but who really are only links in the chain of his plan.

Another type of collective work involves a number of in-dividuals (for example working at the same clinic), each assuming responsibility for a particular problem within a given project. Results represent individual achievements. But the whole which they combine to make up remains a collective aggregate dependent upon conversation and mutual criticism both oral and written.

The continuity of intellectual tradition is represented by "schools of thought." There are two ways in which schools of thought arise. One way is to imitate a master whose work we carry on by extension, adaptation, and analogous achieve-ment. The other way involves an unbroken intellectual tradi-tion, within which the student may be quite as independent as his teacher, since the tradition usually does not center around a single personality but a group. Here we have a school, an intellectual movement which may last through sev-eral generations. Students and teachers who here meet one another on the same level benefit by mutual exchange. Com-petition challenges them to maximum effort. Interest rises in proportion to the response which one's ideas evoke. Competi-tiveness and envy are transformed into an objective and com-petitive enthusiasm.

Schools of thought grow spontaneously; they cannot be induced or deliberately thought up. If one tries to do so, an artificial, sterile activity results. The influx *en masse* of me-diocrity into the learned professions has given rise everywhere to a hothouse culture where either of two things is the rule. Either an external, mechanical method seems easily learned and applied to the point where everyone can "participate," or else a purely formal method of thought together with a limited number of simple axioms can serve as a catchall for just about everything.

New ideas usually originate in very small circles. A few people, two, three or four, perhaps in an institute or clinic, are inspired by the exchange of a common group of ideas which foster new common insights and achievements. Such a spirit grows secretly among friends, proves its value through objective accomplishment; and finally becomes a full-fledged intellectual movement.

The university as a whole can never be united by such a spirit. That spirit belongs to smaller groups. The university is most alive when such groups communicate with one another.

The University as the Meeting Place of Different Disciplines and World Outlooks

At the university all disciplines unite. Their students meet. They are united and inspired by the presence of so many forms of knowledge. Their mutual stimulation leads toward the unity of studies. Left to themselves, the sciences tend to fall apart into a loose aggregate of unrelated units. Their joint presence at the university reawakens a sense of their connection and inspires efforts on behalf of their overall unity.

However, the explicit communication between the sciences rests on a broad foundation of implicit communication. There is a basic attraction of intellectual movements, which even as they clash each acknowledges along with their separate identities.

The will to communicate turns upon everything strange and distant, also upon people who would like to shut themselves up in a world of private beliefs. Those who want to communicate of their own accord run the risk of being put to question because only when they are questioned to the utmost does it become clear whether they are heading in the right direction. This urge to communicate has fundamental consequences for the place of intellectual movements at the university.

To be permeated by the idea of the university is part of a way of life. It is the will to search and seek without limitation, to allow reason to develop unrestrictedly, to have an open mind, to leave nothing unquestioned, to maintain truth unconditionally, yet recognizing the danger of *sapere aude* (dare to know). Some people might conclude from this that only that world outlook which we have just discussed should be allowed at the university, with the consequence that dissenters would be subject to an investigation of their beliefs. This, however, would violate the idea of the university. The university does not investigate the *Weltanschauung* of a potential member. Rather it investigates his professional attainment and intellectual standing. The university keeps itself distinct from sects, churches, and fanatical groups, which seek to impose their own outlook upon others. The university does this because it wants to thrive in freedom only and would perish rather than carefully shelter itself from unfamiliar ideas and withdraw from intellectual conflict where fundamentals are involved.

All the university must require of its members is this: professional and intellectual standing, mastery of their tools, and integrity. It would even admit people who have made what is called the *sacrificio del intelletto* (the sacrifice of the intellect), even those who would be intolerant if they could. The university feels confident that it can afford to do so. It wants to live dynamically, not statically. In its will to communicate it seeks to associate even with those who resist communication. It would be contrary to the idea of the university to deny admission to a man of intellectual rank who shows

proof of intellectual achievement and works in a scholarly way
—even if his scholarship ultimately serves an alien interest.

The demand that every world outlook be represented at
the university, for example in philosophy, history, sociology
and political science, is just as unsuited to the idea of the university. If a given world outlook fails to produce scholars of
the first rank, then this outlook has no claim to scientific
status. The individual certainly prefers living together with
those who share his ideas. As long as he acknowledges the
idea of the university and has a voice in the selection of potential faculty members, however, he will be inclined to draw the
most diverse viewpoints into the university. He does this in
order to create opportunities for fruitful conflict, to broaden
the intellectual range at whatever risk—above all, to allow
scholarly achievement and intellectual quality alone to be the
decisive factors. The university not only tolerates but demands that persons who oppose its aims be admitted to it.
So long as these people are content to state and discuss their
particular beliefs and authorities within the university, so long
as they allow their beliefs to be an impulse for their research,
they are useful to the university. But if they seek to dominate
the university with these beliefs, if in the selection of candidates for the university they are partial to fellow-believers, if
they replace intellectual freedom by prophetic propaganda,
then they come into the sharpest of conflict with the rest of
the university which aims to uphold the ideal of the university.

CHAPTER SIX: *The University as an Institution*

The university fulfills its tasks—research, instruction, training, communication—within an institutional framework. It requires buildings, materials, books and institutes and their orderly administration. Privileges and duties must be distributed among its members. The university represents an independent corporate whole with its own constitution.

The university exists only to the extent that it is institutionalized. The idea becomes concrete in the institution. The extent to which it does this determines the quality of the university. Stripped of its ideal the university loses all value. Yet "institution" necessarily implies compromises. The idea is never perfectly realized. Because of this a permanent state of tension exists at the university between the idea and the shortcomings of the institutional and corporate reality.

The Failure of the Institution to Live Up to the Idea of the University

Even the best institutions at the university are apt to deteriorate and to become distorted. Thus the very translation of thought into teachable form tends to impoverish its intellectual vitality. Once intellectual achievement is admitted into the body of accepted learning those achievements tend to assume an air of finality. Thus, it is merely a matter of convention at what point one subject ends and the other begins. It is possible, moreover, that an excellent scholar may not be able to find a place for himself within the established departmental divisions. A mediocre scholar may be preferred to him simply because his work fits into the traditional scheme.

Any institution tends to consider itself an end in itself.

Though an institutional structure is indispensable to the progress and transmission of research, only constant re-examination
can insure its proper functioning on behalf of the ideal it is
meant to serve. For administrative organizations are notori-
ously intent upon perpetuating themselves.

Ostensibly, the university's vested freedom to select its
own new members favors the choice of the best. In practice,
however, this system tends to favor the second best. Not only
the university but all corporate bodies tend to maintain an
unconscious solidarity against both the excellent and mediocre,
prompted by such anti-intellectual motivations as fear of competition and jealousy. The excellent are instinctively excluded
from fear of competition, just as the inferior are rejected out
of concern for the prestige and influence of the university.
The "competent," the second-rate, are selected, people who
are on the same intellectual level as oneself. This is one more
reason why appointments to vacant professorships cannot be
left exclusively to the departments concerned but must be subject to control by a third party. As J. Grimm has said, "The
state has no business allowing the supervision of academic
appointments to slip out of its hands: allowing each faculty
to appoint its own members would contradict the greater part
of common experience. Fear of competition exerts a certain
force even over men with the most honest of motives."

Fateful decisions are made when the institution selects
new appointees from the younger generation. The university
is by no means accessible to anyone who has made intellectual
contributions. Access is provided by a senior professor—in
Germany, an *ordinarius*—who must sponsor the appointment
before the faculty. Professors are inclined to prefer their own
disciples in matters of appointment, if they do not indeed
limit access to them entirely. On the strength of the sheer
duration of their study under a given professor these students feel that they have earned the right to academic
appointment—a right which they claim unjustly but which

the professor recognizes for reasons of personal sympathy. Professors are sought after who have the reputation of finding academic jobs for their students. Max Weber tried to curb this unwholesome practice by proposing the principle that whoever had taken his doctorate under one senior professor should be required to seek academic employment under another senior man at another university. When he tried to apply this equitable principle to his own students, however, he discovered at once that one of his own students met with flat disbelief when applying for a position at another institution, and that people preferred to believe that Weber had rejected his own student as incompetent.

A professor still incurs grave guilt when he favors his own students by exaggerating their real stature and performance where new appointments are involved. There must be no compromise with the principle that quality and quantity of scholarly production govern the selection of new appointees. Otherwise, the decline of the university is assured. It occurs when a poor appointment policy favors mere studiousness over independent thinking, and substitutes a civil service type of automatic promotion for the risk of securing professional approval by independent achievement. Whereas many teachers tend to favor this sort of studiousness, which is unlikely to upset the routine or offer serious competition, every professor should make it his principle to allow only those students to become members of the faculty whom he can expect to attain at least the same level of proficiency as himself. He should be on the lookout for those who might surpass him, go far beyond him, and to advance these men even if they are not his own students.

Institutions can easily become the tool of scholars who desire power, and use their reputations, connections, and friends to advance certain people more or less ruthlessly. Since Hegel's time the authority wielded by the respective heads of an entire school of thought has been the target of constant complaint.

Free communication which ideally prevails at the university all too often degenerates into a quarrel between conflicting personalities. Jealousy and envy lead to unfairly destructive criticism. Even during the most culturally advanced periods in the nineteenth century such abuses flourished. Goethe recognized this sickness in the university when he compared it with independent research: "Here as everywhere learning advances quietly or dramatically, while those professionally concerned with it are not really interested in it at all but are merely interested in money and personal power"; and "They hate and persecute one another about nothing at all as all can see, because no one wants to tolerate anyone else, although they could all live very comfortably if everyone lived and let live." It is one of the maxims of the sensible university teacher never to acknowledge purely negative criticism or the intrigues which grow out of it, to deal with it as if it were nonexistent, or at least to blunt its impact so that fruitful, cooperative work may continue to flourish in the interests of the university as a whole.

Paradoxically, the unlimited freedom in research and teaching, to which each member of the university is ideally entitled, serves not only to promote that unrestricted communication which exposes everyone to radical doubt, but it also promotes a tendency to enclose the specialist in his field, to make him untouchable, to isolate him instead of encouraging him to communicate. Everybody leaves everyone else greater liberties so as to be entitled to them himself and to be safe from the meddling of others. The conduct of faculty members has been compared with that of the monkeys on the palm trees of the holy grove at Benares: on every palm tree sits a monkey, all seem to be very peaceful and minding their own business. But the moment one monkey tries to climb up the palm tree of another he runs into a heavy barrage of coco-nuts. Similarly, mutual respect in university circles tends to a state of affairs where everyone may indulge his every inclina-tion or caprice, with the result that the university no longer centers on matters of common concern. Common concern is tactfully reserved for formal occasions. Thus it can happen that everybody approves everyone else's candidates for aca-demic appointment simply in order to have freedom in this matter oneself. Basic criticism is avoided. Communication which ought to be an intellectual battle for clarity and sub-stance becomes a purely outward relationship governed solely by considerations of politeness. There is, to be sure, some wis-dom in this: the individual scholar's intellectual productivity must be assured freedom to the point of allowing for what to some contemporaries seem eccentricities or license. Though discussion and criticism must naturally accompany the work of a scientist or scholar, "official" exercise of criticism for the sake of controlling individual research and teaching, whether of professor, lecturer or even student, is intolerable. In all matters extending beyond the personal realm and involving the interests of a department or the university as a whole, mutual discussion becomes a duty, particularly in the case of new appointments. In the personal realm, there is no substi-tute for spontaneous and informal discussion for genuine com-munication in accordance with the idea of the university. It marks the presence of genuine intellectuality of the kind that is no respecter of persons. It is a tragic paradox that academic freedom tends to obliterate this ultimate freedom of true com-munication.

The Necessity for Institutions

These and other shortcomings of the institutional struc-ture do not obviate the need for institutionalization in some form. Without an institution the life and work of the individual scholar are in danger of being wasted. Life and work should become part of a tradition safeguarded along institutional lines so that later generations can profit by them. Scientific achievements, in particular, are dependent on material means which the individual seldom has at his disposal. They are also dependent on the sort of cooperation possible only at a permanent institution.

This is why we cherish the university as institution, why we love it to the extent that it manages to incarnate its ideal. Despite all its shortcomings it is the locus of this ideal. It assures us that a community of scholars can exist. There is special satisfaction in belonging to such an institution, if only for honor's sake. It hurts not to be admitted to it or to be expelled by it.

Students and professors ought not to consider the university as a mere chance institution of society, nor as a mere school, a production-line of necessary degrees. They ought to assimilate the idea of the university, that Western supranational idea, of Graeco-German origin. This idea is not something that can be touched, seen, or heard. It glimmers in the ashes of institution, flaring up from time to time in individuals or groups. One need not always belong to a university to live by its ideal. But the idea is attracted to the institution, without which it feels incomplete, sterile, and isolated. To live according to this idea means becoming part of a larger whole.

All this, however, must not be allowed to lead to the arrogant assumption that the university is the sole and proper place for an intellectual life. We who love the university as the place in which we lead our lives may not forget the special nature and limitations of the university. In many cases what is creative comes into being outside the university, is at first rejected by the university, then adopted, and so on until it comes into its own.

Renaissance humanism grew outside of and opposed to

the scholastic universities. When the universities had become humanistic, then philologically oriented, the revival of philosophy and of the natural sciences in the seventeenth century again had its source outside the university, with men such as Descartes, Spinoza, Leibniz, Pascal and Kepler. When the philosophy of Christian Wolff and his disciples had penetrated the university, a new humanism arose whose chief exponents were Winkelmann, Lessing and Goethe, again outside the university. This humanism, however, quickly conquered the university because of great philologists such as F. A. Wolf. Smaller movements, too, often arise outside the university and are long ignored by it. Examples are Marxist sociology, hypnotism, long since accepted as a recognized field, graphology, just beginning to be taken note of at the university, and introspective psychology as developed by Kirkegaard and Nietzsche. As J. Grimm writes, "Our universities are places where a large and ever-growing book-learning is present. Yet they tend to ignore any radically new piece of work until it has proved its validity elsewhere. Universities are like gardens where wild growths are only reluctantly tolerated." *

Still, once a new intellectual direction has been developed, the university will take possession of it sooner or later, promote further development by new discoveries and application and preserve it as part of its body of teachable materials. Yet it can only teach a subject in which it does independent research. This is exactly what happened at the university again and again. In several notable instances, however, the universities have pioneered new directions of thinking. Foremost among these are the Kantian philosophy and the philosophy of German idealism which followed in its wake. Moreover, throughout the nineteenth century almost all new discoveries in history and the natural sciences originated at the university.

* *Kleine Schriften* (Berlin, F. Dümmler, 1864), I. 242.

The Role of Personality within the Formal Structure of the University

The ultimate problem posed by the institutional structure of the university is the place of human beings in it. For its vitality the university depends on persons, not institutions, which are no more than a physical prerequisite. The university is judged by its ability to attract the best people and provide them with the most favorable conditions for research, communication, and teaching.

Tensions between the living personality of the research-scholar and institutional forms are unavoidable. Where the idea of the university remains vitally alive this results in creative change. Times of conservatism alternate with times of rapid change.

No idea can be realized without being modified. Institutions, laws, and conventions have a way of obtruding themselves. Once the idea disappears, only meaningless routine is left. The things that matter cannot be forcibly brought into being by institutional dictates. It is always dangerous when an institution tries to reproduce artificially something that can only grow organically. The really important contributions are made only by those who commit their lives to the service of truth over an unbroken period of years and decades.

Administrators can be judged by the relative importance they attach to persons or institutions. It takes people to instill life into an institution. The mere survival and continued functioning of certain ancient institutions reflects a deep wisdom. Yet even this wisdom is to a large measure dependent on the quality of its present members. Thus individual personality and institutions are interdependent. Their polarity is never without tension.

Institutions are purposeful mechanisms devised to make the transaction of business safer and surer. They establish those forms which, until altered deliberately, retain unquestioned validity. To abide by these forms and rules is one of the conditions of intellectual work. It provides foundation and order. Formal regulations should be limited to these foundations, and even then be as sensible as possible so as to encourage cheerful compliance until they become second nature. In so complying one actually enhances one's freedom.

In every institution there are differences of rank and authority above and beyond the obvious differences of individual caliber. Rational organization is unthinkable without leadership. The original way was for students to gather around a teacher informally. Today a director of research supervises his institute and assistants in an institutional manner. This is bearable and even desirable only if the man in charge is at the same time *the* outstanding intellect. In permanent institutions that is a matter of luck. What is intolerable is the rule of incompetents who want to compensate for their lack of intelligence and dissatisfaction with themselves by gratifying their power drives. Productive people who have a talent for leadership are excellent for this job. Aware of their own limitations, they will leave their subordinates all possible freedom, in the hope that these go even further than they themselves.

No institution by itself is ever satisfactory. It is corrupted by the addition of complicated refinements of institutional procedure. Simplicity is the most difficult thing to achieve. Premature simplification oversimplifies.

Complex relationships are not resolved but destroyed by "simple" solutions, such as separating research from teaching institutes, pure from applied science, liberal education from specialized training, the instruction of the best from that of the many. Genuine intellectual life occurs only where teaching and research do not simply exist side by side but go hand in hand. This is an ideal which can only be realized by the work of complete persons.

The polarity of person and institution begets opposite errors. On the one hand there is the cult of personality, the emphasis on originality and even eccentricity. On the other hand there is an emphasis on oppressive and empty organization. Both extremes lead to unreasonableness—in one case because of tradition for tradition's sake, in the other because of innovation for the sake of innovation. The university's attitude is hard to formulate: it aims to steer clear of either extreme. It tolerates individual eccentricities, it is receptive to new personalities, and provides a meeting ground of the greatest extremes. Individuals are important even where there is no cult of personality because ideas are realized only through the individual effort of people. There is a sense for rank and merit at the university and a feeling of respect for age. The individual scholar wants to feel welcome among his colleagues, elected by, not forced upon, them.

CHAPTER SEVEN: *The Cosmos of Knowledge*

In origin, the various sciences grew from practical experience, from the art of healing, from surveying, from the workshops of builder and painter, from navigation. The unity of science is a philosophical idea. In practice the philosophical ideal of unity became the search for a single organic body of knowledge. So began the cooperation of all branches of learning toward a common goal.

Practical instruction, dating back to time immemorial, is concerned not with the whole or the purity of knowledge, but only with the particular skill required for a particular occupation. By contrast, scientific instruction in accordance with the ideal of the university seeks to guide us to the foundations of all knowledge by the light of the idea of unity. It encourages a particular skill to uncover those roots which join it to the single whole of science, so that its deeper meaning and full range may become apparent.

The university must always meet the needs of the practical occupations. In this respect it resembles the ancient training schools. But it adds something totally new when it meets these needs by way of defining their place within the whole of knowledge.

Thus, from one point of view, the university resembles an aggregate of professional training schools isolated from one another, or an intellectual department store with an abundance of goods for every taste. But from another point of view, it is clear that this is mere appearance since, if true, the university would simply disintegrate. The very existence of the university stands for that oneness and wholeness of all knowledge which alone enables us to know in the broader sense of the term.

The wholeness of knowledge, however, presents us with the task of classifying all knowledge. The departmental divisions appear to but do not in fact coincide with this classification. Though they can never really coincide they must be related to one another.

The course catalogue of any large university will suffice as a first guide to the kinds of different subjects in existence. We find that the university is divided into faculties and these in turn into departments divided by subject—in almost endless variety. Clearly the course catalogue as a whole is the product not of a master plan, but of a slow process of historical accretion.

The Classification of Knowledge

Since the idea of knowledge as a cosmos does not stem from practical application but from philosophy, its vitality is tied to the diffusion of philosophical awareness throughout the university.

From the very start, the idea of knowledge as a unity has given rise to different systems of classifying the various fields of knowledge. Classifications abound. None of them, however, can claim absolute truth and validity. Definitive classifications have always reflected someone's proud conviction of having hit upon the whole and absolute truth of things.

As "absolute" truths definitively formulated here and now have succeeded one another, the necessary relativity of all systems of classification has become increasingly clear. Our faculty of understanding has been emancipated. The educational power of knowledge has ceased to be identical with a fixed world outlook and ontology. It is replaced by our realization that our capacity for learning new things is infinite.

To assume that one has the one final and correct classification of studies is to pretend that a given field of knowledge can be defined and localized with the help of certain fixed, absolute points. Conversely, to attempt to relate a given field to the whole of knowledge involves pushing inquiry to those depths where that field appears as a microcosmic replica of the whole of knowledge. For there is almost no significant fact which is not at some point related to the whole of knowledge in that it is either illumined by its context or itself in turn illumines that context.

Knowledge is usually classified according to some pair of opposites. Thus there are:

(1) Theoretical and practical studies. Theoretical studies are concerned with a given subject as an end in itself; practical studies are concerned with the subject as a means toward the realization of practical ends.

(2) Empirical sciences and purely rational sciences. Empirical sciences deal with real objects in space and time. Pure sciences deal with concepts which are intelligible once they can be independently derived. Mathematics is unique among the sciences in that it deals solely with ideal objects.

(3) Natural sciences and cultural sciences. The object of empirical sciences can be grasped in two ways. It can be grasped from without like matter or understood from within like the human mind. The natural sciences explain things from without through laws of causation or mathematical constructs; the cultural sciences or humanities understand from within by ascertaining purpose and meaning.

(4) Sciences concerned with general laws and historical sciences, the former seeking the universal, the latter, the particular and historically unique.

(5) Basic sciences and auxiliary sciences. Basic sciences seek to learn by reference to the whole of knowledge, hence become representative of the whole and therefore universal in character. Auxiliary sciences either collect material or assemble knowledge for a particular practical purpose.

In each of these pairs the opposing principles of scientific understanding complement one another. They can but briefly isolate themselves, for in isolation each becomes sterile. In practice, each pair of opposites asserts itself simultaneously, there being no way of dividing them neatly and permanently into opposites.

The concrete sciences are united only by the object which they seek to approximate with every method at their disposal. They no more fit into a fixed classification scheme than do the widening and intersecting circles caused by pebbles tossed into a pool. But then these widening circles may conceivably be classified according to the relative nature and position of the pebbles involved. Thus, sciences may be ranked in the order of their intrinsic priority where each level depends on the next lower one, as in the order physics, chemistry, psychology, sociology. This would be a series of sciences seeking the universal. Or cosmic history, world history, life history, human history, European history. This would be a series of studies concerned with what is unique and individual. Whatever our system of classification, it is always predicated on a single pair of opposites and to that extent not all-inclusive. Further examination would show that such schemes can never illumine more than single sciences, and imperfectly at that; that genuine classification is unattainable. At best, a given scheme has pragmatic relevance to a specific area of actual research.

Usually the unity of any given scheme is furnished by that particular science which this scheme favors. There is good reason for the fact that almost every science has at one time or another declared itself the only genuine, all-inclusive and absolute science. The reason is that every true science constitutes a single whole. Error ensues only when the wholeness of one science is allowed to obscure the equally autonomous wholeness of other sciences. One-sided emphasis on a particular science impoverishes science as a whole.

The unity of all knowledge is an ideal. Every classification is a provisional attempt to translate this ideal into reality from a particular point of view and in terms of a particular intellectual and historical situation. To that extent every scheme is false.

Academic Departments

No single principle governs the organization of disciplines at a university. No one man has planned this classification with the knowledge of the whole picture in mind, as in the case of industrial division of labor. On the contrary, there have arisen a number of separate intellectual movements each aiming individually at the whole of knowledge. The particular sciences have remained such independent wholes. They do not lie next to one another like the separate drawers of a filing cabinet, but overlap, and interrelate without necessarily intermingling. They communicate without blurring into one another, guided by the vision of an infinitely large single body of knowledge. The essence of the university is concerted yet unregimented activity, a life of diversity yet inspired by the ideal of wholeness, the cooperation yet independence of many disciplines.

Departmentalization still in use today dates back to the medieval period. The three upper faculties were theology, jurisprudence and medicine. A fourth or lower faculty was added—the liberal arts, today's philosophical faculty. (The meaning of these faculties has changed as the meaning of research has changed. For the last 150 years the number of faculties has at times been increased, then again reduced to the old number. Today there are usually five, because the old philosophical faculty has been broken up into two faculties, one of mathematics and natural sciences and one of liberal arts.)

These faculties claim to mirror faithfully the cosmos of

sciences. They represent the whole of human knowledge. They arose from the practical needs of intellectual work, not from theoretical schemes of classifying the sciences. The continuing validity of these faculties today, after centuries of radical change in our environment, our knowledge, and our research, attests to the truth of their original conception. Theology, jurisprudence and medicine cover permanent areas of inquiry: understanding of religious revelation, of statute law, both private and public, and of the nature of man. The study of these subjects is meant to train ministers, judges, administrators and physicians for their practical careers. They all need at least logic and philosophy as a common foundation.

The sciences of theology, jurisprudence, and medicine aim for an end itself no longer scientific, the eternal salvation of the soul, the general welfare of people as members of society, and bodily health, respectively. Paradoxically then, these sciences originate outside the scientific realm. They work with assumptions which though themselves not scientific, impart substance, meaning and purpose to science. Theology is concerned with revelation approached in three ways: through the history of the holy scriptures, through the church, through dogma, and verified in terms of contemporary faith. Jurisprudence is concerned with rationalizing and standardizing statute law as produced and validated by the power of a given state. Medicine is concerned with preserving, fostering and restoring the health of human beings, and is based on an inclusive knowledge of human nature.

Each of these scientific disciplines is entirely based on nonscientific premises. Each must seek to shed light on these premises. For without them it loses all meaning, as shown by the following typical phenomena.

Theology touches upon the supra-rational realm but through rational means. Now, instead of rationally developing the meaning of revelation, theology can develop a passion for "the absurd." Self-contradiction is then supposed to confirm the very truth of an assertion; the enslavement of reason to confirm the very truth of faith; and arbitrary submission to an authority, even though in reality it exists in the world in the form of judgments and expressions, which are supposed to be the true way of life. Brutality, fanaticism, inquisitions, and lovelessness—these make up this theological fury.

Conversely, revelation, the basis of faith, may be lost. Faith is then equated with rational doctrine and deduced from reason alone. But as revelation, the historical foundation of faith is lost, faith itself is lost. Reduced to unrestricted rational thinking, it ends up in unbelief.

Jurisprudence bases itself upon the reality of the positive legal order. This order of statute law is to be made meaningful, coherent, and consistent. Natural law, though by no means a fixed standard, provides a guiding idea of what is right or wrong. Without this foundation, jurisprudence sinks into the abyss of total arbitrariness. Statute law then is valid simply because backed up by state power. Self-contradiction and injustice cease to be valid counterarguments. Illegality is legally sanctioned, and thought itself bows before the law of force.

Conversely, a jurisprudence concerned only with natural law and without any reference to actual statute law becomes meaningless too.

Medicine is premised on the will to advance the life and health of all men as human beings. This ideal admits of no qualification. First and foremost, the desire to help and heal concerns itself with individuals. It concerns large groups only in so far as individuals profit, and no individual is physically harmed.

Yet, medical interest in health is as ambiguous as the concept of physical health itself. The task of medicine involves conflicting tendencies. It becomes meaningless both where the individual's inalienable right to physical health is abandoned, and where the meaning of physical health becomes a convenient but overly simple stereotype.

Once a particular racial or physiological type is preferred to man as a whole, a motive exists for doing harm to the life and health of individuals for the supposed benefit of some particular group as a whole. Thus, persons presumed to have large chances of transmitting unfavorable hereditary traits have been forcibly sterilized, and in the name of euthanasia the mentally ill have been murdered.

In the three so-called higher faculties, the ideas of reason, natural law (justice), and life and health are standards indispensable to research, if it is to retain any meaning. But in revelation, positive law, and human nature dark powers remain which we can endlessly illuminate but never fully understand, and it is these that endow research with substance and life.

The philosophical faculty enjoys a unique position. Originally, it did not prepare for a specific profession but prepared solely for the higher faculties (theology, jurisprudence and medicine). Today, the function of the philosophical faculty has changed from a preparatory to a fundamental one. The philosophical faculty embraces all other branches of knowledge. The three remaining faculties derive their intellectual substance from contact with the basic disciplines comprised in the philosophical faculty (the faculty of arts and sciences). Thus from the viewpoint of research and theory alone, the philosophical faculty by itself comprises the whole university. Any classification of knowledge which includes everything contained in the philosophical faculty is complete.

In the course of the nineteenth century, the philosophical faculty lost both its uniqueness and its unity. It split up into a faculty of mathematics and natural sciences, on the one hand, and humanities, on the other, from which, in turn, a social science faculty branched off. One came to think of the faculties as existing side by side rather than forming an organic whole. In this way, the idea of the oneness of the university was lost. The university became an aggregate, an intellectual department store.

Several motives entered into this split-up: the size of the old faculty which included more professors than all the other three faculties combined; the schism between the natural sciences and the liberal arts which entailed estrangement, lack of understanding and mutual disdain; and the need to train people for different professions such as teaching, chemistry, physics, geology, and agriculture.

The reunification of the university, which stems from an awareness of the cosmos of the sciences, cannot simply mean restoring things to their medieval unity. The whole content of modern knowledge and research must be integrated: broadening the scope of the university must initiate a genuine unification of all branches of learning.

The Expansion of the University

In the modern world the university keeps establishing institutes and teaching organizations designed to meet the changing requirements of society. Thus, areas of specialized technical training or entirely new curricula for professional courses of study require special ways of teaching. Nothing can stop the continuing expansion of the university. This process has meaning, because all human activity involves knowledge. Wherever there arises a demand for knowledge the university is responsible for forging ahead in the new field and teaching it.

Not infrequently the net result was a meaningless aggregate of totally unrelated fields. Astronomy and business administration, philosophy and hotel management find themselves equals in this intellectual "department store."

To ignore the presence of these newcomers is nothing but useless snobbery. The idea of the university requires that the university be open to new ideas. There is nothing which is not worth knowing about, no art which does not involve a form of knowledge. Only by unifying these various new lines of inquiry can the university do justice to them. The university is called upon to preserve the scientific spirit by transforming and assimilating the new materials and skills and integrating them in the light of a few leading ideas.

There are two ways in which the curriculum may be broadened by increasing the number of subjects offered. On the one hand, science differentiates itself in the natural course of its growth. In this process each new phase remains an integral whole comparable to the propagation of life. In this way, psychiatry as well as ophthalmology achieved an independent status within medicine itself, because they developed both subject matter and scientists of universal significance. Conversely, legal medicine does not qualify as an independent field, but is a collection of technical skills and "know how." Similarly, the status of dental medicine, as well as the medicine of ear, nose and throat, is dubious because the organs concerned lack universal implications. These fields lack the over-all significance of internal medicine, psychiatry or ophthalmology. Public health, too, enjoys a dubious status. Although outstanding representatives of this field have rightly held professorships, the field itself has its practical and technical limitations; it lacks a really challenging idea. The mere fact that people working in the field of public sanitation have made contributions to bacteriology does not suffice to enroll public sanitation in the ranks of the basic sciences. To give detailed answers to the questions raised here would require further study and expert knowledge in the fields concerned. We are here concerned only with the principle: the split-up of sciences into new fields of study is desirable to the extent that a given new field can, in turn, develop into an integral whole in touch with universal ideas and so remain a basic science.

Alternatively, science can grow if new materials and skills enter into it from without. They demand admittance because they can make a valuable contribution to the cosmos of the sciences. Thus, for example, the content of the cultures concerned explains why Indic and Chinese studies are basic sciences; African and prehistoric studies are not.

Whenever the university expands it must keep its sights set on the unity of knowledge, on the daily task of revalidating this unity, in two ways. Throughout all change, the university must retain its awareness of the basic sciences and of the hierarchy both of basic as against auxiliary sciences and of instruction through research as against mere factual and technical instruction.

The expansion of the university is a problem which relates to its very survival in the modern world. New ideas must be recognized and made part of the whole of the university. It is yet to be seen whether the university is equal to the new world, whether it can accept it and serve it, whether the new knowledge and the new abilities can be permeated with the spirit without which they are, strictly speaking, meaningless.

Theology, jurisprudence and medicine, traditionally the three upper faculties, address themselves to areas of human existence that have remained unchanged for thousands of years. Nonetheless, they do not cover the whole of modern existence. This is evident if one considers the large variety of institutions of higher learning which have been founded outside the confines of the university itself, such as technological institutes, agricultural colleges, veterinary colleges, teachers' colleges, schools of business administration, schools of mining, etc. Is their mere existence not proof that the life of the university has failed in important respects? Does not the establishment of these independent institutes violate the idea of the university?

It is significant, indeed, that these establishments tend to duplicate some of the work of the university, that they have a natural tendency to expand into a university so that, for example, we find all the liberal arts, up to and including philosophy, being taught at technical institutes. More often than not, however, even the presence of outstanding scholars in the humanities has not been able to produce anything more than an empty educational routine bereft of the vitality and strength which comes only with creative scholarship. Thus, these scholars frequently feel as exiles. Could it be that there is some connection between the growing emptiness of modern life and this growth of diverse specialized schools? Is there a way which would lead back from the superficiality of specialism, the general aimlessness, the dilemma of diverse special schools, to some new unity? Whatever possibility exists hinges upon the extent to which vast new areas of human life can be incorporated in the university. Medicine, jurisprudence and theology, the three traditional branches of learning, no longer suffice as they did for the medieval world. Yet, progress cannot be achieved by simply increasing the number of departments. One cannot just add a new department whenever a new field has been opened up somewhere on a large scale. Even highly specialized departments must relate to a genuinely important sector of human life.

This is not a new idea. In 1803, for example, the local government established in Heidelberg "a department of political economy" and incorporated it temporarily into the philosophical faculty. This department included forestry, urban and rural economics, mining and surveying, civil engineering, architecture, assaying, and police organization, "everything that concerns the knowledge, preservation, development and proper maintenance of public administration." All that eventually remained of these arts and sciences was what came to be known as economics. Clearly the department failed to encompass a genuine self-contained sector of human life. The reference to public administration served as a utilitarian catchall for various unrelated jobs, but failed to provide a unifying ideal.

Yet, here were the roots of an important later development, which became a factor in the public mind only gradually in the course of the nineteenth century. This is technology, which, as is becoming ever clearer, is the sole really new field. Although technology is ages old, and has developed through thousands of years, until the end of the eighteenth century it remained a part of handicraft. Hence it remained basically unchanged and part of man's daily life within his natural environment. Then, during the last 150 years, technology made an incision deeper than all the events of world history over the past thousands of years, as deep perhaps as that caused by the discovery of tools and of fire. Technology has become an independent giant. It grows and advances. It brings about a unified and planned exploitation of the globe, an exploitation which is financially profitable. Trapped in the spell of technology, men seem no longer capable of controlling what originated as their own works. Technology has a claim to our basic concerns equal in objectivity to that of theology, jurisprudence and medicine, a claim which was not fully recognized until it compelled our attention amid the catastrophic changes and events of recent history. For it is technology which has now taken over the job of molding man's natural environment, of transforming human life even as it transforms nature and the technical world.

To expand the university by creating a fourth faculty next to the three upper faculties, theology, jurisprudence and medicine, poses a real challenge. Technology represents an entirely new and developing area of human life. Unclear as is the ultimate effect of technology upon human existence, it is involved in a development at once planned and chaotic.

We all observe the drastic changes of our immediate environment. Apartment house and public building, road construction and traffic management, transportation and communication, the furnishing of kitchen, desk and bed, the supply of water, gas and electricity—all of which spell the difference between our modern environment and earlier ones, are held together not only by utilitarian considerations, or by the agency of the natural sciences, but by the novel concept of man's transformation of his natural environment.

Still, this novel conception of human life and the enormous apparatus dedicated to its maintenance have so far failed to crystallize into a controlled and permanent pattern. The restless march of technological change on a gigantic scale makes us stagger between ecstasy and bewilderment, between the most fabulous power and the most elementary helplessness.

Everything seems to flow into the one great stream of technological organization which for reasons which escape adequate historical understanding began to flow 150 years ago and to this day continues to swell steadily, flooding everything. Today, we feel that this colossal phenomenon must stem from metaphysical sources, that all must accept its objectives at pain of extinction. It seems as if there is something that is bound to awake even though still half asleep, something that until now has remained silent behind the great mass of ingenious technological devices, something dimly perceived by a few individuals like Goethe and Burckhardt who reacted to it with a mixture of horror and distaste.

Perhaps, the best interests of the intellectual life as well as of technology are served by making the university their mutual meeting place. Perhaps then, technology and the confusion which has resulted from it would be infused with meaning and purpose. Perhaps then, out of the idea of the university would grow an openness, truthfulness, up-to-dateness in which this idea would prove itself. Thus the university would in effect be transforming itself.

Only a revival of the old idea of the university could make scholars feel the magnitude of their task to the point where the creation of a new technical faculty would benefit the university as a whole. But the university as a whole would have to share in this rededication if it is to have a chance of promoting a general rebirth. The university's great task would be to create a truly comprehensive awareness of our age in terms of the sum total of knowledge and practical skills of which the integration of the technical faculty is only one aspect.

Along with the incorporation of a school of technology other changes would become essential. Above all, the old philosophical faculty must be reunified. The division into the natural sciences and the humanities must be overcome. Only reunification can impart sufficient force to the basic theoretical disciplines to counteract the increased impact and scope of the practical disciplines. This reduces the danger that its continued isolation at the university will slowly drive the natural sciences into the camp of technology and medicine, leaving the other faculties to cherish precious memories in aesthetic isolation without vigor and relevance.

More than that, it would necessitate reintroducing into the sciences the concept of hierarchy, which distinguishes between basic and auxiliary disciplines.

A technical faculty would be something new at the university. It would have to be more than just a new faculty or school. It would have to get the university to do something entirely new. The university must face the great problem of modern man: how out of technology there can arise that metaphysical foundation of a new way of life which technology has made possible. It is impossible to predict which disciplines will provide the strongest impulses to this end, once scholars and scientists have begun to realize this task in close and constant intellectual cooperation.

Technology is an autonomous discipline which like any other field is prone to certain grave and specific errors once it loses sight of its own presuppositions. Thus, theology was shown to be prone to lapse deliberately from the secret of revelation into absurdity and witch hunting; jurisprudence to lapse from its concern with statute law into legal rationalization of lawless brutality and licence; medicine to lapse from its essential duty to heal, to euthanasia and the killing of the insane. Similarly, technology either does or does not live up to its ideals. We have heard about inventors who in their old age were overcome by horror at the realization of the evil they had unwittingly and indirectly brought about by their discoveries. We have heard about the emptiness of certain kinds of technical work, the arbitrary nature of its goals, the pointlessness of mere competence as such. Yet the foundation of all technical activity is the profoundly informed will to develop more fully man's existence in this world.

A technical faculty can serve no more than the medical one as a mere annex to the philosophical faculty. It has its own independent area of existence and its own practical task. Still, like medicine it is grounded intrinsically and pedagogically in the basic sciences which are part of the philosophical faculty.

The following are the most immediate consequences of the proposed change: as the university absorbs the institute of technology, the need for duplicating physics, chemistry and mathematics is removed. The history of ideas, history of art, economics and political science would also become part of the philosophic faculty. The needs of technology would impart fresh life to the philosophic faculty as a whole. For the basic disciplines would more consciously focus on the common horizon of theoretical inquiry. Their teaching would be directed to the common problems of medicine, technology and teaching. It is difficult to say how this will manifest itself in the personality of the individual scholar. Quite possibly, teaching will stress the historical development of scientific and mathematical insights and in this way carry over the unity of the philosophical faculty into the individual sciences.

All told, both university and technical institutes stand to profit from unification. The university would grow richer, more inclusive and more modern. Its basic problems would be infused with new life. Conversely, the technological world would become more contemplative as the problem of its meaning becomes a matter of serious concern. Its self-affirmation and its limits, its over-optimism and its tragic disappointments would all be placed in a deeper context.

It is exceedingly important, however, to recognize the independence and universality of the technical world as a modern phenomenon without drawing the empty conclusion that a great many other departments are warranted by the same token. In no case can the study of agriculture, forestry, business administration, etc., be considered as faculties of equal status with the technological faculty. These are specialties, pure and simple, without a truly comprehensive subject. Still they must not be excluded from the university. The university is free to teach whatever is teachable provided it distinguishes sharply between research subjects and auxiliary subjects such as those mentioned above. Research subjects cover disciplines whose content and level of achievement merit incorporation into the university itself. The other group of subjects does not merit incorporation, but affiliation only to the university, at least for the time being. Their teachers and students will work in the atmosphere and framework of the university without belonging to it in the narrower sense.

The university faculty member differs from the teacher of affiliated subjects (like agriculture, business administration, etc.) in that he is judged not only on his teaching performance but on the merit of his self-directed research. The faculty member engaged in research differs from his technical assistant in that he is concerned with the basic problems and their meaning. The technical assistant limits himself to the collection of facts, auxiliary work, and certain well-defined preliminary objectives.

A higher education is a prerequisite for an ever-growing number of jobs. We have the choice of either ignoring this need from a misplaced and unrealistic sense of caste or else of doing something to help meet it. If we choose the second path (carefully and step by step, as is only reasonable) the difficult question arises whether there really is a long run need at the university for isolated "service" skills. We have to decide if our common interests are really served by specialized intellectual techniques, a kind of second order manual labor, a mere routine efficiency without a corresponding vision of the whole; or if this is pernicious in the long run, even though, for the time being at least, we must learn to put up with it. Does the university embody the aspirations of *all* men and is it therefore called upon ultimately to accept all applicants and to elevate to a higher level each and every branch of human knowledge and technique? Or does it contain an esoteric element, forever intelligible only to a minority?

We must not allow ourselves to be deceived by the inevitable demands of those who oppose the idea of intellectual hierarchy. Their claims are premature. Equality of intellectual status cannot be decreed. It can only be earned through patient and individual effort and growth. Nor must we be deceived by the dream that all people can achieve the noblest function of humanity. This is a utopian dream which is not realized simply by assuming that it exists already when, in fact, no one knows or is capable of knowing to what extent it can be realized. A temporary solution is that the university set up schools which are affiliated with but not actually part of the university. The university must maintain its aristocratic principles if it is not to fall prey to a universal lowering of standards. The actual incorporation of affiliated schools into the university is not a matter of decree. It can only be accomplished by allowing these schools to grow into intellectual maturity in their own way. If this is done, then the actual incorporation is no more than a formal recognition of an accomplished fact.

PART III: *The Requisites for the Existence of the University*

In considering the idea of the university we must consider certain realities which are simultaneously prerequisites and restrictions of that idea.

First, there are the human beings who come together at the university, their attitudes and abilities. (Ch. 8)

Second, there is the power of state and society, whose will and needs sustain the university. (Ch. 9)

CHAPTER EIGHT: *The Human Factor*

All of university life depends upon the nature of the people participating in it. The character of a given university is determined by the professors appointed to it. Every university is dependent upon the kind of persons it can attract. The truest idea of the university is all in vain if the people who could realize it are no longer around. If these people exist, however, it becomes a question of life and death to the university to find and attract them.

University life is no less dependent on students than on professors. The best professors flounder helplessly at a school where the student body is unfit. Hence, it is all up to the young people who are supposedly entitled to study. They must show themselves worthy of this privilege to the best of their ability. Admission to the university must be determined through some process of selection. For admission some preparatory schooling is necessarily required; without this, study at the university would be futile. Further, the person seeking admission must be educable, that is, he must have the capacities, talents and characteristics which can be developed through study at a university.

There is the question as to the kind of student to which the university addresses itself: outwardly to all, intrinsically to the best only. Its aim is that the best in the growing generation may be able to develop freely. Yet who will turn out to be the "best" cannot be determined beforehand. It is difficult, moreover, deliberately to produce or sponsor a specific type without perhaps slighting the most capable, that is, the most serious group of students, those who are most deeply involved with truth as an ideal. For such people study and research are not mere drudgery or simply one occupation among many others; rather, the privilege of helping to create new knowledge and serve the cause of truth is to them a matter of the most vital and personal concern. Thus the "best" cannot be defined in terms of a single type. They represent a great variety of individuals who have identified their life and innermost being with the objective achievement of truths and results.

The intellectually oriented person is typically committed to the intellectual life—not as a means to something else, some external purpose, or worldly success, but for its own sake. Thus, he strives within his particular professional situation to realize and perfect a given professional ideal (such as doctor, teacher, judge, etc.), to infuse each sphere of life with its requisite measure of human integrity and each phase of intellectual work with the clear awareness of its underlying meaning. When relieved from concern with the immediate exigencies of life such a man will utilize his leisure in the disciplined pursuit of problems of intrinsic value. If his very life is an end in itself it is so only because it coincides with the fulfillment of an objective intellectual task the awareness of which imparts a deep sense of human satisfaction. Manifestly, the best are selected not so that they can be used as human raw material for ends unrelated to their own human fulfillment, but so that their very intellectuality may help them achieve their proper individual humanity as an end in itself.

The problem of selecting individuals from among a great variety of human types falls under three heads: (1) what aptitudes are desirable? (2) how are they distributed? and (3) who is to make the selection?

Types of Aptitude

In our experience, people are both very different and very much alike. Whoever demands equal rights for all is thinking of what men have in common. This demand is valid where common ground and equality really exist, as in material existence and its needs. To stress the differences between men means to demand that qualitative difference between men be recognized and respected. To this group belong those who recognize the various aptitudes and desire their most effective employment; who take note of human interests and drives, of the different degrees of commitment to the life of the mind and of the ability to sacrifice on behalf of this life.

The differences among people are truly extraordinary. For anyone prepared to face facts this is an inescapable insight. Practical experience and tests confirm it. At the same time, man is intrinsically a being with unlimited possibilities open to him. For strictly speaking, the individual as a whole can never be classified according to a given talent or character type. All such attempts illumine only aspects of him, never the whole. Three distinctions may conveniently be made. There are (a) the variables of aptitude: memory, the ability to observe and learn, resistance to fatigue, amenability to training, sensory equipment, ability to distinguish differences, the power of concentration, speed, etc. All this is experimentally verifiable and more or less testable. Whole groups of individuals can be graded so as to select those best fitted for certain aptitudes.

(b) Intelligence proper is harder to get at. Various techniques have been tried to test ability to see relationships, adaptability, and judgment. But their results are far less reliable. Though clearly reliable at times, they can surprise us with apparent evidence to the effect that otherwise unpromising people seem to show considerable intelligence in one specific area. There is an ambiguity of emphasis on special talent, on the one hand, and general intelligence, on the other, without a final decision in favor of one or the other.

Then there are (c) spirituality and the ethos of intellectual commitment—those factors which can neither be experimentally grasped nor studied empirically with any degree of finality. They are intelligence in the sense of personal commitment, motivation (apart from the pleasure involved in performance, in succeeding and in out-performing others), devotion to one's work, nobility of mind, truthfulness, and enthusiasm for learning. These qualities are always rare even among the examiners who make the actual selection and who frequently are themselves only poorly endowed with the spark of intellect so defined.

(d) Creativity is wholly inaccessible to objective testing. It is given to some and may either be developed through hard work or wasted through disregard. There are numbers of depraved geniuses who waste their gifts through lack of discipline and good sense. Genius develops only where it is matched by commensurate commitment, will power, application, and craftsmanship. There are highly gifted people who eventually lose everything and degenerate intellectually. So long as the flame of genius is tended it produces basic insights, ideas and forms. It cannot be produced at will, calculated, bred, deliberately favored in selection or enforced in terms of standards. Unlike talent and aptitude, it cannot be inherited. Metaphysically speaking, genius is an experiment, a conjecture of absolute mind; it is the source of all intellectual change. We live on the insights obtained for us by genius and made available to everyday understanding. Our highest respect is due to genius even where it is wasted. It is up to us to perceive real genius, to bring it to light, to make it felt. Here is a task we can deliberately undertake: to assimilate the work of genius. However great the difference between genius and ourselves there is an impulse of genius and basic insight in every person—especially in youth; we are concerned with it because somewhere we too are of its kind. There is an absolute difference between genius and everything else which is only talent and good will. Still, nobody is entirely a genius, only a human being with genius. This fire burns more or less brightly in all people. No man is a god. But the difference in degree is so tremendous that we have a qualitative basis for feeling our distance from genius. The decisive difference between people is whether this demon rules their lives or whether they are primarily governed by a social, occupational and ethical order alone.

In distinguishing aptitudes, intelligence, spirituality, and creativity, we are prone to the fallacy of misplaced concreteness, by thinking that ability is something definitely given.

In the first place, the character traits that appear in terms of aptitude cannot be grasped the way we grasp simple concrete objects, for they are the human factor par excellence which is only partially accessible to objective psychological techniques. To a very large extent character and aptitude remain accessible only to the philosopher willing to face the transcendental, "encompassing" aspect of man. Psychological aptitude tests are not meaningful beyond the level of purely external characteristics. There simply are no objective criteria by which the "encompassing" can be measured or tested.

In the second place, no person is ever entirely in agreement with what his outward appearance indicates. Just as an entire people may appear changed if the traditional ruling group is displaced by a new human type of hitherto obscure and subservient standing, so an individual can become an entirely different person when a new environment of language and gesture fosters hitherto unfamiliar elements of his personality. Any particular realization of human possibilities is no more than fragmentary by comparison with a man's full potential; it is a highly selective rearrangement favoring a few specific possibilities.

In the third place, man is the source of his own decisions. At some point every man makes a decision concerning himself. The phrase "But I'm made that way" is only a device of evading one's freedom.

There nevertheless exists a broad inventory of human qualities which cannot be changed and must simply be accepted. But one cannot be careful enough when pronouncing certain character traits final or postulating that certain talents are biologically inherited. I do not doubt that these exist and exert a profound effect in terms of offering certain possibilities or excluding them. But we have not succeeded in identifying these traits precisely, except where they fall within the limits of conventional testing procedures. One judges people altogether too easily. The scientific study of character and ability is a matter of serious and lofty interest. But in the last analysis, we know clearly that we do not know. This is precisely why we must leave room for education and the demands man makes upon himself.

Education affects those people most significantly who have not made up their minds about themselves. How we are brought up from earliest youth is all-important. Not only a person's fixed, testable aptitude is decisive, but also unforeseeable possibilities, whose realization always destroys other possibilities. The dominant spirit of a home, an institution, a community, can be recognized through the behavior and way of speaking which the group adopts, through symbols and phrases unconsciously acknowledged, through group standards and conventions. To judge a group of people by their appearances is always unfair if one does not take into account the education which has been and continues to be part of their daily lives. To learn more about their true potentials, though never all, one would have to see what would have become of them under a different upbringing. The whole courage to educate derives from a trust in such dormant potentialities.

Though no man can ever know once and for all who he is and what he can do, he must try himself out. Serious personal commitment, verifiable only by one's conscience and not to be delegated to the pressure of outside opinion, must be one's sole guide. I cannot know beforehand what I can make of myself through hard work and resolute commitment. Fichte actually advises against self-examination of one's abilities. Those able to enter a university should think of themselves as scholars-to-be. Since one must always strive to live up to the standards implicit in a given situation, at the university one must consider oneself called upon to do the very best one can, as a matter not of privilege but of obligation. All told, people are not fixed species which can be made use of or not like animals. They constantly change and develop because they are full of hidden possibilities.

The Distribution of Aptitudes and the Characteristics of the Masses

All societies contain differences not only in material welfare, but—above all and unavoidably—in rank. Ideally, the best are also the leaders, so that the social hierarchy coincides with the hierarchy of personal excellence and aptitude. This was Plato's ideal. Social conditions would not improve until philosophers were statesmen, or statesmen philosophers.

This ideal cannot be completely realized, for everything human is in flux, and no realization can last for more than a moment. There are two reasons for this. Opinions change as to which personal values are the most important ones. Various talents become more or less useful according to the sociological, economic, and technical world situation. Moreover, every difference of competence is quickly frozen into formal status. For without permanence and continuity, life could not go on. It does not matter greatly if this status is inherited, or passed on from teacher to pupil. Those that follow after the original group of creative leaders tend to become epigones, possessing rather than creating tradition and losing the original spirit.

Thus, the ideal itself is exposed to corruption. It must, therefore, rely on the ablest of any generation to fill the leading positions. Sociological differences themselves demand that such a selection take place. Whether it occurs spontaneously or deliberately, it is unavoidable in any case. Many are the forces that effect this selection. The goal of fair distribution of educational opportunity is achieved only in limited areas of selection. The ideal that every man get his due, learn, and work, according to his natural capacities, is attained not even by the greatest and happiest of men. Ideally man is infinite, though harnessed to finite conditions. He is human only to the extent that he acknowledges these conditions. It is up to each man to accept his limitations and to achieve freedom within them. Limitation is a matter of inheritance and ability. Man lives in a time scheme and cannot do everything at once. He is as limited as his life. His native equipment imposes insurmountable limitations. Nonetheless, he is aware that he is free. Restriction is a matter also of background and sociological circumstances. Yet these very restrictions open up new opportunities. Here, too, the person of caliber will refuse to give up the last vestiges of freedom.

As he struggles to realize himself, each man insists on this freedom in the face of limitation and coercion everywhere. When I gather certain facts in order to promote the best possible selection of persons to receive higher education, I break down some of these sociological barriers.

Facts in this sense for example are the sociological background of intellectual leaders in a given historical period. Thus one can inquire into the social origin of outstanding men. Of famous Germans from 1700 to 1860* whose biographical sketch takes up two or more pages in the *General German Biography*, 83.2 percent came from the upper classes, while 16.8 percent came from the lower classes, their families being manual workers, farmers, or proletarians. Of those who belonged to the lower classes 32.7 percent became artists, 27.8 percent academicians, 14.6 percent ministers. The remaining professions are represented by very small percentages. Throughout those centuries the margin by which the lower

* According to Maas, "Über die Herkunftsbedingungen der geistigen Führer," *Arch. f. Sozialwissenschaft*, vol. 41.

classes outnumbered the upper classes was tremendous. German culture was sustained by a few tens of thousands of people as distinct from the remaining millions. It does not, however, follow that the upper classes are more talented by nature. All one may conclude is that the upper classes enjoy a more favorable balance of those educational opportunities which are the condition of supreme achievement. Conversely, however, it would be rash to assume that aptitudes are equally distributed among all social classes, the only differences being those of opportunity. If biological qualities can be modified by selective breeding, then innate differences of ability between sociological classes with a long unbroken tradition are entirely conceivable.

Intrinsically, man is not simply "born." It is not a matter of indifference into what family group or class one is born. His human substance is a product of native endowments and history. Children from families who for generations have kept alive a cultural tradition are intrinsically different from other children. The neglects of childhood can never be made up. Thus, people who in their youth have come in contact with the nobility of Hellenic culture will retain a spark of its vitality for the rest of their lives; they will retain a sense of graceful elegance, a feeling for quality and a perception of spiritual greatness which otherwise they might never have had. Even the greatest intellectual creations are in some way dependent on the individual's experiences as a child. There is something plebeian about Fichte—despite the high flight of his genius—and there is in that genius a streak of fanaticism and narrow-mindedness—the counterpart of social servility.

Tradition alone must not be the only or even foremost criterion for selection. But truthfulness and justice require that the value of tradition in shaping the individual be recognized. In our time irreplaceable treasures of tradition were thoughtlessly squandered. One could hear such misleading opinions as: "The past was all glory and doom. Today we are concerned with something which all can understand and take part in." All true and good. Obviously, a given tradition cannot be presupposed in the case of a person who has no tradition in his background and yet must be brought to self-realization. It is he who will have to be brought *to* the tradition, even though as an adult he will assimilate it differently than he would have done as a child. Even at its best, "general education" cannot by itself convey man's primary thirst for knowledge. Protracted study, the training of generations, the tradition of a cultivated family, all enter into the process of personal growth. Yet, neither schooling, even if available to all, nor the kind of material comfort which allows a lucky few to try a number of things one after another are decisive by themselves. What matters most is informed firmness of purpose and self-discipline. Membership in a family of such traditions is no automatic asset. It can be made an asset if paired with a corresponding sense of obligation. Privileged social status is no automatic asset either. During the past fifty years, materialism, the craze to own everything, proud of its price but with no respect for its intrinsic value, has been far more in evidence in the upper classes. Gone is the traditional background of so many outstanding men: the Protestant parish house, nobility, and the patrician upbringing. There is no artificial substitute for them.

Another "fact," comparable to the sociological factor just mentioned, is the quality of the average person, the great mass of people—elusive as that quality may be. All selection is from this mass, and taken as a whole even a ruling class is such a mass. By an amazing consensus of history, the qualities of any mass have been held in universal low esteem. Most people tend to think of themselves as endowed with more than ordinary gifts and only in times of trouble avail themselves of the excuse that they have no ability in a given direction.

As regards intellectual matters, most people vacillate between arrogance and lame excuses. They strive to seem

stronger than they really are. Thus they naïvely seek to re-
make the world from the ground up, uncritically expecting the
world as a whole to turn just, harmonious and happy. Instead
of supervising their own growth with the strictest self-
discipline, and doing their duty, they run away from both in
obedience to something they call an "idea" and indulge in the
profoundly unintelligent raising of uncritical demands. Solidarity of interests exists not only within a given class, but also
and instinctively among those of average ability. The mass is
hostile to excellence. The mass, recognizing its own incompe-
tence, may raise up and exalt a leader so as to effect a general
leveling and just as easily betray him again. Instinctively, the
average man maintains that political equality extends to intellect and ability. To be sure, there are people who acknowledge their own shortcomings and who act accordingly.
But precisely this is an indication of greater stature. A person
with strong intellectual motivation may be hampered by his
imperfect initial equipment, but if he has genuine enthusiasm
and willingness to sacrifice he must be allowed to follow his
calling.

The Process of Selection

The factors which, apart from any deliberate screening,
inherently and indirectly govern the selection of candidates
for university study are extremely complex.

Formerly, "free competition," supposedly favoring the
"survival of the fittest" was held to be the best form of selection because it is the most natural. What was overlooked is
that any given contest is decided not so much by intellectual
ability and interest as by special aptitudes. Thus, when examinations are the sole criterion, success becomes a matter of
will power and ability to master the required body of facts.
Thus, among adults who in their own spare time have successfully prepared for university entrance and have even gone

on to doctoral and post-doctoral work, there are also those who have never risen above mechanical memorization and who despite encyclopedic knowledge have never felt the breath of genuine intellectuality. Having gone out for success alone, they have converted their entire personality into a tool toward that end.

Moreover, selection may indirectly depend on one's willingness to assimilate the *Weltanschauung* of a group, membership in which confers status. To achieve status in such a group, the individual has to conform both inwardly and outwardly. It soon becomes impossible to dissociate oneself from the role one is playing. Those who most scrupulously conform to the approved pattern make the best careers. Here, too, specific aptitudes rather than real intelligence are the decisive factor: such as a willingness to be regimented, to make concessions, to show aggressiveness or conciliatory indecision— depending upon the group one is trying to please.

Both processes of indirect selection illustrate the effects of the presence or absence of rewards set by society on intellectual achievements. So long as intellectual life brings no tangible rewards, social or economic, only those fired by an uncompromising determination will turn to it. To the extent, however, that education and scholarship carry privilege, they become popular with the mass of people. Since most people seek whatever promises privilege and prestige in excess of their actual capacities, social and economic premiums do not actually favor intellectual achievement, but only its external trappings. The human type preferred by the mechanism of rewards is one without interest in anything for its own sake, in leisure and contemplation, but only in the sterile alternation of "working hard" and "playing hard." To such people everything is but a step up and means to an end: to acquire the social and economic rewards of success with an appetite which increases endlessly.

The realization that such are the mechanisms of selection

can make anyone a pessimist. Yet, the thought of the mere accident of birth demands that we succeed in selecting and
attracting the right kind of person for university study. All
too quickly we assume that selection must be according to
ability, and that such ability must and can be objectively determined in each individual case, and that selection shall be
direct and deliberate rather than indirect and accidental.

In any case the truly great individuals cannot be selected
and identified in advance through tests. "We have to accept
the fact that although ordinary talent is measurable, uncom-
mon talent is difficult to measure and genius not at all"
(Grimm). For the sake of the truly great, living as they do
counter to their times and environment, there ought
to remain enough elasticity in our institutions to allow for the
unpredictable and the risks of radical innovation. Total organization and an inflexible selection machinery would entail
standardized performance for set goals—and soon lead to pa-
ralysis. The life of the mind would vanish. The institution
would become the absolute and final arbiter of everything.

The great men, however, who feel the severity of life
more than others since they must constantly fight for an existence that fits no pre-existent patterns and traditionally makes
them the victims of witch-hunts, are the exception. Selection
as a technique of approximation indispensable for sociological reasons remains a meaningful problem.

Even then we must not forget that every selection is in
some way an injustice. We delude ourselves when we think
that we can avoid such injustice through rational and determined effort. In correcting the injustice done to one party,
we unavoidably cause new injustices to other parties.

Since it is impossible to reach a final solution in this problem of selection, we must deliberately retain a sense of the
infinite potentialities of human nature. Those whose judgment and decision are responsible for the selection must so
exercise their responsibility that they neither obstruct the few

with outstanding talent nor favor the mediocre and inferior, the ambitious and demanding, or the false and pretentious.

Direct selection can be effected in any of three ways: (1) through examinations; (2) through personal selection by someone of higher rank than the applicant; (3) through election from below by a specified group of people.

As for examinations, they are either entrance tests to determine if a person is qualified to study, or they are final examinations to certify that a person has completed a course of study. Supposing that from a large group of people a mere handful is to be selected for study at a higher school or university. Some people will be fascinated by the idea that psychological experiments can objectively determine who the best are. A technique of determining aptitude in advance of actual training, of predicting a person's true potential, would certainly be extremely important. Yet what can we actually test? First and foremost, potential intelligence; actual intelligence only within certain limits—nothing more; potential achievement and available tools, but not quality of mind, creativity, will power, and selflessness. If ever a "selection machine" were to be built whose purpose was to determine an individual's entire future, we should have reached the polar opposite of freedom and free will, which are indispensable to the life of the mind. Man would be trapped in a situation quite as deterministic in its own way as heredity itself, except that it would be far harder to put up with depending, as it does, not on a mysterious destiny, but on human beings who very likely are not even properly qualified for their job. Testing—as a technique supplementing the personal judgment of men of experience—is mandatory only if a particular profession requires the type of aptitude that can be tested.

Early selection for admission to higher education is unavoidable, since today such education can be made available only to a fraction of the whole population. To demand higher education for all persons of ability is to give educational opportunity to the able among the whole population, not just among a few social strata. It also means refusing to obstruct genuine ability by overspecialized testing procedures.

Any entrance requirement is bound to build up inhibitions on the part of potential applicants, particularly if the intellectual values involved are hard to grasp anyway. It is more than likely that there are aptitudes which cannot be tested, that the life of the mind thrives on "slack" and the ability to move about freely, and that the more rigidly an institution is controlled, the greater are its anti-intellectual tendencies.

Final examinations, too, like entrance examinations, can be used for one of two different aims. Either they certify the attainment of normal proficiency in a given field, all but the incompetent being allowed make-up exams in case of failure, or they can be used to screen out all but the top students— possibly even a previously fixed number (*numerus clausus*).

As for selection by ranking individuals, this is difficult to institutionalize since only few people have the necessary qualifications. Cases in point are the monarch who elects his advisors, the teacher who selects his assistants, the university administrator who in his professional capacity must discover those best suited for appointment. Actually, personal selection is the surest and justest way, because it reaches those deep-lying qualities which escape all measurement. This is true, however, only in those rare cases where the person in charge of the selection has an inherent desire to serve and gives himself freely and objectively to the task of deciding about human worth and aptitude, without allowing private prejudice to offset his judgment. In most cases, however, alien motivations are allowed to displace this judgment at once most personal and most objective. When corporate choice replaces individual choice, there is a tendency toward the mediocre. There have never been more than a gifted few who, having an eye for the true substance in man, were truly qualified to choose.

As a rule, professors tend to favor their own students and disciples. They instinctively tend to sidetrack talents and intellects superior to their own. Conversely, there are a few professors who from their very awareness of this danger fight their own preferences and sympathies to the point of lapsing into a kind of partiality in reverse and appoint those whom they do not really want at all. Here again the selection will be poor, even incomprehensible. Finally, and this is probably the most common situation today, the question of need becomes the dominant motive of selection. Human beings are evaluated only as means to an end. The personal stamp which inevitably characterizes intellectual existence is pushed aside as "immaterial," yet not in favor of some higher "matter," but simply in favor of certain tangible, external criteria of fitness to fill a specific need.

Sometimes, by sheer luck, the indefinable art of selecting the right people is actually practiced. This may occur in a hospital where an atmosphere of mutual trust prevails between the director, on the one hand, and the chief physician and his staff, on the other. In situations such as these organizations develop a characteristic spirit of their own. The tactless and the incompetent are quietly dropped. The rest are given elbow room. Decency and dependability set the tone. Thus, by a combination of good luck and individual authority an area has been created where intellectual work of importance can freely be accomplished. It is easier to achieve this within the framework of a clinic than of an entire university; within a select group of one's own students than within an entire faculty.

Whoever is in a position where he must personally select candidates must first of all familiarize himself with the candidate's published work so as to evaluate its true significance. Secondly, he must evaluate the candidate in personal discussion with him. This is easy where both candidate and examiner think along similar lines. But it becomes difficult and ceases to carry conviction where the candidate's cast of mind seems strange, and there is as yet no common ground of work and shared enthusiasm. It may still be possible to listen from afar through perceptive reason and thus to decide if the candidate has something valuable to contribute. In any case, the examiner must be open-minded and not lazily confine himself to familiar standards. Next to objective intellectual attainment he would do well to consider every indication of the personality of the candidate, from physical appearance to handwriting.

Thirdly, there is the possibility of selecting new appointees by majority vote. Either the students elect their own teachers, or the teachers themselves elect new faculty members by co-option. While corporate bodies must resort to co-option, there is no such need for the election of professors by a vote on the part of the students. Nothing good can come of a situation where the judges will be elected by the very persons over whom they will sit in examinations. It would always work out in favor of the "easiest" men. Next, students would subconsciously let their judgment be swayed by such external characteristics (or lack thereof) as sex-appeal, didactic ability, stage presence. The great mass of people always fall for the best showman. There is, to be sure, a minority of perceptive young people with an unerring eye for the teacher's competence, command of the material, stimulating powers, and even intellectual rank. Instinctively, they recognize what is genuine. Yet, only rarely will young people of their kind command the majority necessary in elections.

Clearly, then, all three techniques for selection—examination, personal selection and election by majority vote—have their shortcomings. They are as unavoidable as they are unreliable. They will have to be stripped of their aura of absolute finality in order to leave room for the unusual person. Examinations will, of course, remain indispensable as certifications of competence. Yet, the university is interested in examinations only to the extent that they increase the educational opportunities open to intellectually active people. This interest is only indirectly served by improving the quality of examinations. By ceaselessly improving examinations and making them more meaningful intellectually, we can improve imperceptibly the institutional procedures of selection.

Only the average student benefits from a long series of examinations pacing his course of study. Independent minds will always prefer a single examination at the end of a long period of free study. Their cause is benefited if the university requires all its students to be independent and self-reliant. Only these students are mature: they need no master because they have taken themselves in hand. They expose themselves to doctrines, viewpoints, surveys, facts, good counsel, only in order to examine and decide for themselves. The university is not the place to look for step-by-step guidance. Real students have initiative; they can set their own problems. They can work intellectually and know the meaning of work. They are individuals who deepen their individuality through communication. They are not the people as a whole, not the average, not the mass, but numerous individuals who risk being themselves. This is at once reality and necessary fiction. It represents an unattainable ideal and at the same time a challenge to live up to one's highest aspirations.

University study is terminated by the single examination. Its nature is supremely important. Basically, it is only meant to confirm what has already taken place: self-selection on the part of the students through the exercise of their freedom. The university would cease being a university if a properly qualified student body were shepherded through a fixed curriculum subject to periodic control by examinations. The very nature of the university demands, instead, that the individual exercise his own choices throughout his entire course of study at the acknowledged risk of ending up with nothing. Hence, our most serious and ultimately insoluble problem is how to create an intellectual and institutional climate at the university favorable to such independence. First and foremost, there is the task of improving the final examinations. They must be simplified and broadened at the same time: simplified by limiting the fields covered and by reducing their number, broadened by calling upon the entire intellectual energy, judgment and ability of the candidate.

The examinations must proceed from a real assessment of the student's conduct and achievement in seminars and other forms of group work. Mere evidence of industry and grades are unimportant. There must be tangible proof of achievement. Good written work ought also be submitted and should also be taken into account.

In the examination itself attention must be paid, not only to factual knowledge, but to the candidate's conduct, his approach to a given problem, the type of methods he uses, his ability to see things, his ability to write and speak in a manner appropriate to the subject matter at hand.

Requirements may change in accordance with the number of applicants and the demands of certain professions. If a high general level of achievement is reached, the standards of selection are bound to be correspondingly high. In every case, the candidate must remain aware that he may, after all, fail to pass in the end.

As to their subject, the examinations ought to be largely dependent upon the candidate's own choice. The fiction of encyclopedic knowledge must be abandoned. Care must be taken that the examiner's teaching habits do not subject the candidate's freedom of study to their pet schemes, making success in the examination dependent upon familiarity with specific lectures and seminars given by the examiners.

Through mutual exchange of experiences and viewpoints universities must consciously develop and improve their examining techniques. Even though the examiner's skill counts for most, systematic improvement is possible. The psychology and philosophy of education must keep us in touch with the qualities both of talent and training necessary for the learned professions.

Finally, examinations and grades must be given as rarely as possible. The more numerous they become, the less responsibly can they be administered. If they are few in number, they can be administered with seriousness and with thoroughness. The busy routine of tests and marks combined with excessive factual coverage comes to nothing because this kind of examination has ceased to be truly selective. Despite their routine character they place an undue burden on the professor's time and lower the general level of the intellectual life.

CHAPTER NINE: *State and Society*

The university exists through the good graces of the body politic. Its existence is dependent on political considerations. It can only live where and as the state desires. The state makes the university's existence possible and protects it.

The University as a State within the State

The university owes its existence to society, which desires that somewhere within its confines pure, independent, unbiased research be carried on. Society wants the university because it feels that the pure service of truth somewhere within its orbit serves its own interests. No state intolerant of any restriction on its power for fear of the consequences of a pure search for truth, will ever allow a genuine university to exist.

Having exempted the university from interference by its own power, the state respects the university and protects it against all other forms of interference. The university is meant to function as the intellectual conscience of an era. It is to be a group of persons who do not have to bear responsibility for current politics, precisely because they alone bear unlimited responsibility for the development of truth. Though outside the world of practical affairs, the university as a place of research is necessarily permeated with a sense of reality. Knowledge, not action, is its link with reality. Value judgments and practical action are suspended in favor of the ideal of pure truth.

A life away from the arena of practical affairs is meaningful only if sustained by a passion for learning and understanding. It is an inward form of activity; a series of triumphant acts of self-discipline. Yet the academic life, once entered upon, is ever prone to its own set of corruptions, which threaten to muddy the pure atmosphere of intellectual activity. Suspension of value judgments may degenerate into mere neutralist indifference; suspension of practical action, into laziness; intellectual caution, into neurotic fear of any challenge to enfeebled energies.

Changes in the University in a Changing World

Society provides the university with legal and material support so that it may function as a center carrying on basic research for the benefit of all and affording people studying for the professions an intellectual climate as well as practical training. Thus, the university is continuously serving the needs of state and society, and bound to change as society and the professions change.

During the Middle Ages, it had to train the clergy, later on the higher government officials, the doctors and the teachers. Until the seventeenth century, knowledge of God, theology and philosophy had been the all-important subjects. Since then, however, the growing influence of technology has increasingly called for specialized training. The most recent and sociologically inevitable stage has been the admission of women to university study. Over the past fifty years, the number of occupations requiring university study has been steadily increasing. The corresponding increase in university attendance, a factor beyond the control of all concerned, has brought about a change in attitude on the part of all members of the university, and particularly in the relations between teacher and student. Steady growth of enrollment has changed the nature and function of the university imperceptibly during the period from the nineteenth century to the First World War and more so ever since. To meet this new call for mass education, the university has been forced to adopt the methods and procedures of the high school.

Yet society affects the whole spirit of the university not only indirectly but directly and deliberately through political means. This type of influence has changed drastically from one historical period to the next. Unfortunately, Humboldt's advice to governments never to think of themselves as indispensable has gone unheeded except for a few rare and notable moments in the joint history of university and state. State interference has always meant favoritism for particular sets of beliefs. This has been true of monarchies and to a lesser degree also of parliamentary types of government; under radical regimes and dictatorships such interference tends to the point of outright violence.

Influences both political and sociological transform the university. Yet behind its many changing forms looms the timeless ideal of intellectual insight which is supposed to be realized here, yet which is in permanent danger of being lost. The historical conflict between this philosophical impulse and society's ever-changing demands is marked by alternate periods of fruitful cooperation, each in its own way unique, and periods in which the philosophical ideal suffers utter defeat. Hence the alternation of periods of sterility with periods of vitality. One way in which the university itself can lose out is by excessive concessions to outside pressures for mass education and by lowering its standards to the high school level. The public influence enjoyed by the university has been similarly subject to fluctuations.

The Meaning of Government Supervision

As a corporation with official charter, the university runs itself, yet is simultaneously responsible to the state that charters and protects it. Legally, therefore, it has a dual status full of ambiguity and even tension. While the university can never become "a state within a state" in the full sense of the word, the converse, its degradation to the rank of a public institution bereft of all individuality, is quite conceivable.

As a matter of fact, the relations between state and university are almost always tense, often marked by open conflict. The state has easily the upper hand over the university and can in fact destroy it. For without the state the university is helpless. Hence, all conflict must confine itself to the intellectual plane. The initiative must come from the mind and spirit manifested by the university which must compel the public mind to clarify its thinking and discern its proper objectives. It must eschew clever political maneuverings as not only inappropriate but fatal to its integrity. It must frankly and openly show what it stands for. It controls the state through the power of truth, not of force. The outcome of this intellectual conflict will, then, be the cooperation of state and university, not the destruction of the weaker by the stronger party—always assuming, of course, that the state does want to help realize the idea of the university. If it does not, the university has no choice but to keep alive its ideal in secret, to refrain from all public activity and await the eventual fall of the present regime. Even so, the university is lost if official hostility to its ideal should persist over a long period of time.

Assuming the cooperation of state and university, let us look at some concrete examples of what state supervision involves. First of all, the state will implement its concern for the independence of universities by acknowledging certain legally binding forms of that independence. The university as a corporate entity must be certain that it is independent. Thus, the professor is not primarily a civil servant but a member of a closed corporation. The civil servant merely carries out the political decisions of higher authorities. He is duty-bound to obey, as a judge is bound to existing laws which he may only apply. His virtue consists in carrying out instructions to the letter. By contrast, the professor's essential work is of his own choosing. He is duty-bound to assume personal responsibility for his own research activity all the way from the initial problem he poses himself without any outside interference. He makes his decisions on the basis of criteria immanent in his work, which elude outside prediction, instant verification and final judgment. The professor must, first and foremost, think of himself as a research worker and teacher, not as member of a corporation or as a civil servant.

The state merely functions as the ubiquitous overseer of the university's corporate independence. The university, in turn, freely acknowledges this function, neither secretly rejecting the underwriter of its independence as a necessary evil nor obediently bowing to every whim of the state. It confidently accepts state supervision so long as this does not conflict with the cause of truth. Loss of this confidence spells disaster. For state supervision may at times protect the university against acts harmful to the true ideal of the university itself. And if the state should make improper demands upon the university, the university has the duty to speak up and clearly state the intellectual principles on which it bases its objections. For it is this formulation of its ideal on the part of the university which enables the state to come to know, so to speak, its own mind and act accordingly. The university, in turn, achieves self-knowledge only as it achieves objectivity.

The task of overseeing the university carries with it grave responsibilities for the state. Any man so charged ought, I think, be equipped above all with a sense of intellectual quality and an attitude toward the intellectually creative people entrusted to his care comparable to that of a horticultural expert toward precious plants. He must subordinate all considerations to the task of discovering and cultivating the kind of intellectual vitality which can only be recognized and cultivated but cannot be "made," and must be ever ready to combat all opposite tendencies. In all matters of intellectual culture, inseparable as they are from human character and personality, the overseer's great power must never be used to undermine the moral integrity of professors. There have been times when universities gained in the visible accessories of glory such as institutes and endowments what they lost in professional integrity. When approached with contempt, treated with disrespect, maneuvered into situations which virtually impose unethical conduct, and exposed to academic politics in the most literal sense, professors, like the rest of mankind, will eventually respond in conformity with the worst expectations. Administrators are always tempted to place exclusive emphasis on mere externals and immediately visible results; they are tempted by the feel of power, by the craving for recognition and gratitude. Professors, on the other hand, incline to flattery and docility in order to get ahead. Ideally, discussions between administrator and professor are frank and on a high level of moral integrity. Disappointments are bound to occur frequently. But the spirit of an administration is judged by its aims and expectations, not only by its instances of disappointment.

In character and attitude the overseer or trustee of a university needs a different endowment than that of a professor. He must face present realities with detachment and objectivity, yet respect individual personalities. He must without vanity derive satisfaction from knowing that he has contributed to the flowering of a world not of his own making, but under his care and dependent on that care. He has to try to evaluate the quality of intellectual life on behalf of which he must make financial decisions to the best of his ability. All this requires a high and sovereign detachment. In general, professors cannot fulfill this particular requirement. Working in particular fields and therefore easily partisan, they are intellectually committed to special interests and therefore are not sufficiently detached. There are exceptions, of course. But since the tasks and necessary talents of administrator and professor differ as they do, one does well not to allow former professors to act as overseers and trustees over other professors. People with legal training, administrators by training and choice, are preferable. Were professors ever to indicate that they wanted only professors in administrative posts, this would have to be strenuously opposed. At the very least, the overseer who lives in the same place as the university of which he is responsible ought never to be allowed to lecture. His work must be confined to the wholly separate sphere of administrator.

The purpose of state supervision is precisely to prevent those corruptions to which a completely independent university would be exposed. Fear of outside competition and of excellence tends to turn self-administrative bodies into monopolistic cliques interested in safeguarding their own mediocrity. Inevitably, the promotion and hiring pattern will then reflect a gradual and almost imperceptible lowering of standards. The system of co-option by itself will fail to produce ever better men and will instead favor a mediocre common denominator.

However, if and when political interests interfere directly with university life, then state administration becomes a threat to the university. It is incompatible with the idea of the university that the state demand any more direct services from the university than to supply professionally trained people. Hence, it is disastrous if the state demands something which only serves the purpose of political propaganda. Any state interference with teaching cannot help violating the idea of the university. This danger remains even when the state must interfere to take disciplinary action against university members abusing their position for overt political ends.

The state has a direct stake in education since it wants civil servants, doctors, ministers, engineers, chemists, and the like. But it must be left to the university to decide how this training is to be accomplished to get the best possible results. The state must confine itself to a purely supervisory capacity. Thus, while on continental Europe doctoral examinations must conform to state-set standards, they, at the same time, are administered solely by the universities. The state cannot interfere with their intellectual content except to the extent of enforcing the standard, whose maintenance is required by the idea of the university itself.

The Principle of an Intellectual Aristocracy

In 1930, the American Abraham Flexner wrote as follows: "But democracy is a social and political, not an intellectual possibility, beyond the fact that to the aristocracy of intellect every individual should be eligible on the basis of ability without regard to any other consideration whatsoever." *

Two problems are involved here. First there is the principle of intellectual aristocracy itself, on which is based the hierarchical structure within the university. Secondly, there is the toleration by democratic society as a whole of that minority which this principle involves. The second problem is the one stressed by Flexner. It comes down to a problem of politics.

Intellectual aristocracy is not aristocracy in the sociological sense. Everyone born into the intellectual aristocracy should be given a chance to attend the university. This aristocracy has a freedom that is self-achieved and includes men of noble birth, workers, the rich and the poor. But it is always rare and confined to a few, a minority.

Majorities have always been hostile to privileged individuals and minority groups. Their hatred for the rich, for the gifted, and for a cultural tradition, is always great. Most of

* *Universities: American, English, German* (New York: Oxford University Press, 1930), p. 338.

all, however, they hate anyone basically different from themselves, anyone moved by that genuine and uncompromising will for knowledge which the great majority never experience, yet feel compelled to acknowledge as a noble challenge. The incompetent cannot rise to meet this challenge because of a deep-seated failure of will. By contrast, people with a calling for the highest will love and quietly revere those of noble mind and spirit and translate this love into increased demands upon themselves.

Hence, whenever majorities are politically decisive, a dual process of selection is continuously at work. On the one hand, people instinctively reject those with an original and uncompromising intellect. Secretly everyone agrees that great men are a public catastrophe even though officially the call is for men of caliber. What people want is men of normal ability. Men of below average ability, on the other hand, lose out just as men of outstanding talents are quietly sidetracked through the countless little acts of the majority. How, then, explain that social groups ruled by the majority do in fact support minorities committed to the search for knowledge in their midst? The Middle Ages believed in the delegation of corporate functions so that the philosopher in contemplating God was active on behalf and in representation of the great mass of people, who were fulfilling different corporate functions. The masses of our time probably no longer believe in this delegation of corporate functions. Today, they might justify the existence of science and scholarship by claiming that because "science is a good thing" (a belief which certainly underlies the whole popular cult of "science") it must have an assigned place in society where it can work freely and take chances without the constant pressure for useful results. The problem remains, even if society believes in this firmly enough to restrain its otherwise irresistible momentum toward assimilation and collectivization, whether this leviathan will itself agree to respect the place of scholarship and science. Will society agree to reserve a place for an understanding beyond its comprehension, yet of potential future utility?

The Search for Truth and Its Relation to Politics

Politics has a place at the university, not as actual struggle, but as an object of research. Where political struggles invade the university, it is the idea of the university itself which suffers. Since the existence and external form of the university are dependent upon political decisions and good will, there is no room within the confines of the university, free from state interference by state consent, for political conflict and propaganda, only for the quest for truth.

This means that the university requires absolute freedom of teaching. The state guarantees the university the right to carry on research and teaching uncontrolled by party politics or by any compulsion through political, philosophical, or religious ideologies.

Academic freedom extends not only to research and thought but also to teaching. For thought and research need the challenge and the communication which teaching affords and which in turn depends on the freedom of scholars and scientists the world over to speak and write as they please. The state is determined to grant groups of scholars and scientists the facilities for the kind of long-term mutual exchange which they require for a balanced view of their subjects. In the study of man's nature, mind, and history, even the most extreme intellectual possibilities are to be explored to the fullest not only in the form of casual, random and quickly forgotten intuitions, but in the disciplined continuity of major intellectual productions. Only thus can we preserve in ages of intellectual barbarism those elements of knowledge and culture which can again become an inspiration to broader masses of people in happier times.

Academic freedom proves its value wherever there are people who have merged their personal with their intellectual existence. They become the representative minds of an epoch when their very awareness of historical forces frees them from the obvious and trivial kinds of dependence upon their time.

All men are potentially capable of meditation and reflection. But only a very few have the calling for intellectual work in all its complexity. This minority includes the members of all professions requiring university study. It is the only group which can respond intelligently and critically to the advancement of learning. Though the search for truth does not produce benefits of immediate tangible use to the public at large, the public itself wants this search to continue as a free, long range proposition, on behalf of the nation as a whole.

Not every state is interested in truth to the point of granting academic freedom. No state anxious to conceal a basic criminality of principle and action can possibly want the truth. It is bound to be hostile to the university, pretending friendliness only the better to destroy it eventually.

Academic freedom means the freedom of student and teacher to do research in their own way and teach as they see fit. As for actual subject matter, that the state leaves up to each individual. This defines the very freedom which it guarantees against all interference, including its own. Academic freedom resembles religious freedom to the extent that each of these freedoms is guaranteed not only against state interference but is so guaranteed by the state itself.

Academic freedom can survive only if the scholars invoking it remain aware of its meaning. It does not mean the right to say what one pleases. Truth is much too difficult and great a task that it should be mistaken for the passionate exchange of half-truths spoken in the heat of the moment. It exists only where scholarly ends and a commitment to truth are involved. Practical objectives, educational bias, or political propaganda have no right to invoke academic freedom.

Academic freedom and constitutional freedom of speech only superficially resemble one another. For it is quite conceivable that academic freedom may continue even after the constitutional freedom of speech has been abolished.

Faculty members cannot invoke their constitutional freedom of speech except as private citizens. They cannot expect the university with which they are professionally affiliated to come out in their support when they speak as private citizens. They are entitled to this protection only in matters relating to professional publication, but not in connection with casual political remarks, opinions, or newspaper articles. Academic freedom does not entitle them to special privilege over other citizens. It means the professional freedom from all obligations other than intellectual thoroughness, method and system. It does not entitle one to irresponsible pronouncements on public affairs. On the contrary, it obliges one not to cloak such casual pronouncements in a false air of authority, to be doubly careful about making them in the first place.

There is, of course, a long-standing tradition of professorial intervention in politics. Most of it is not very glorious. Instances to the contrary are rare and atypical. The seven famous Göttingen professors dismissed in 1837 for political dissent left their posts not because they dissented politically, but because they felt unable to reconcile their religious convictions with the breaking of the oath they had taken to the constitution. Max Weber was the only and inimitable exception to the rule. His political statements were themselves part of his intellectual achievement. Democratic contemporaries labeled them "high brow" and written above the heads of his audience. As for Socrates, never once during the twenty-seven years of war with Sparta did he take sides in the hotly debated issues of the day except after the battle of the Arginusae, when he alone among the group blocking the unconstitutional vote to execute the generals refused to sacrifice ethical principle to popular pressure and give in. With this single exception, Socrates spent his life probing his fellow citizens with questions aimed at their most basic motivations and so made himself more disquieting to them than the worst demagogue.

Where expert knowledge is involved in contemporary issues, scholars and scientists have the right to make pronouncements. They can apply their knowledge through the medium of medical, technical and constitutional opinions. They can systematically apply their knowledge to any contemporary problem which in the eyes of state and society appears important. The form in which they make their contribution felt is through rational argument rather than personal intervention. Their task is to restate the evidence and to provide a clear picture of the total situation. They are free to volunteer this information even though normally they ought to speak out only in reply to direct inquiry. In practice, however, every answer to contemporary problems is likely to be biased by nonobjective considerations. The very questions are apt to be loaded. No critical scholar should ever forget how close he is, when faced with questions put to him by the public, to the position of the priest in Hebbel's play, who is told by Holophernes to find reasons for a decision already made.

Academic freedom is not a piece of property to be owned and enjoyed once and for all. The very economic dependence implicit in salaried status harbors a latent threat to the professor's moral integrity. Inevitably, professors tend to support the social conditions which favor them and give them status; to recognize the existing state of affairs and to serve the current government with their spoken and written word. The publicly appointed professor has come in for more than his due share of distrust, ever since Schopenhauer leveled his grotesquely exaggerated charges against state-salaried philosophy professors. Such mistrust is justified only when it takes the form of self-criticism. It is no accident that ever since Socrates

quite a few philosophers have thought it important to remain
entirely independent and refuse reimbursement in any form
whatsoever.

The University and the Nation

Greek in origin, the idea of the university is part of the
Western tradition.

As a publicly endowed institution the university belongs
to the state; as a privately endowed institution it is certainly
part of a given national scene. In either case, it is the expres-
sion of a whole people. Seeking truth and the improvement of
mankind, the university aims to stand for man's humanity par
excellence. *Humanitas* is part of its very fiber, no matter how
often and how deeply that term has changed its meaning.

Thus, while every university is part of a nation, it has its
sights set on goals above and beyond nationhood. Differences
aside, in this respect, at least, it is akin to the idea of the
church. The university proper must not take sides in the conflict between nations, even though as human beings its members have each their national allegiance. Members of the university, whether faculty, deans or the president himself, abuse
their position if they should choose to hold political rallies in
favor of either a particular party or of the country as a whole.
They serve their nation and all mankind solely through the
medium of intellectual creativity. The idea of the university
suffers when abused for extraneous ends. Nationalism, like
everything else, forms a legitimate topic of research but cannot
provide the basic direction of the university itself.

❖   ❖   ❖

We have come to the end. Beginning with the attempt to
define the nature of science and the intellectual life sustaining
it, we were led to examine the university as an institution.

The variety of issues which had to be raised could obscure the one all-important issue: the ideal of the university which is the very lifeblood of higher education. This ideal cannot be reduced to a few simple statements but had to be brought out indirectly. May we grow ever more aware of its real meaning, and may it serve as a standard guiding our judgment of all aspects of university life. No one who does not feel its validity can be made to see it. Since discussion is fruitless except where there is common ground, all we have done is put familiar facts in a new light.

We are deeply committed to this ideal which has given meaning to our life; yet we lack the necessary strength to speak of it with the enthusiasm it deserves. We know that truth, striving all around us to be seen and recognized, will live or perish with our ability to realize the ideal of the university in its ever-changing forms.